THE ISLAMIC AND CHRISTIAN CALENDARS

Dinumerare nos doce dies nostros,
ut perveniamus sapientiam cordis.

PSALM 89, 13 (NEW LATIN VERSION).

O *teach us to number our days:*
that we may apply our hearts unto wisdom.

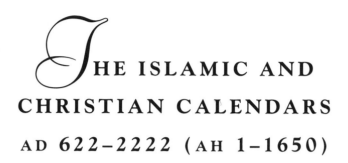

THE ISLAMIC AND CHRISTIAN CALENDARS

AD 622–2222 (AH 1–1650)

A complete guide for converting
Christian and Islamic dates
and dates of festivals

G. S. P. Freeman-Grenville

Garnet
PUBLISHING

The Islamic & Christian Calendars

Published by Garnet Publishing Ltd
8 Southern Court, South Street,
Reading RG1 4QS, UK

First English edition 1963
Second edition 1977

ISBN 1 85964 066 4

British Library Cataloguing-in-Publication Data
A catalogue record for this book is available from
the British library.

Jacket and book design by David Rose
Typeset by Samantha Abley
Printed in Lebanon

TABLE OF CONTENTS

INTRODUCTION

❖

This is a new version of my *The Muslim and Christian Calendars* (1963, 1977), which is now out of date. The revision takes both Islamic and Christian dates up to AD 2222. The original was written primarily for eastern Africa, and has been altered to meet a wider demand, and to emend errors in the earlier printing.

I am grateful to many scholars who have corresponded with me from time to time. I am particularly grateful to the late Dr J. F. P. Hopkins, who checked the tables when – to use his own words – he was 'seized by computer mania', and whose results are now in the Cambridge University Library; I am particularly indebted to R. W. Bailey, who has helped me greatly with his computer in the additional parts of the work. I am likewise grateful to Helen Brown and Sarah Searight for friendly prods.

This book contains the equivalent of any date or day in either the Islamic or the Christian Calendar from the first day of the Hijra up to the Christian year AD 2222. It is possible to calculate the date of any future festival in either calendar.

On the representation of Members of the British Parliament, it has been proposed to fix the date of Easter. This proposal was accepted by the late Pope Pius XII, as well as, for the Church of England, by the Archbishop of Canterbury. The matter is one of current international negotiation, and it is possible that the Christian Calendar will be changed within the present generation, and the date of Easter fixed. When this has been done, TABLE EIGHT will be out of date.

G. S. P. F-G
SHERIFF HUTTON, YORK
1 June 1995

One

THE ISLAMIC CALENDAR

❖

The Moon revolves round the Earth in 29⅓ days. But because the Earth is itself in motion, this revolution in fact takes just over 29½ days. The Earth itself performs a complete revolution once in twenty-four hours, and at the same time revolves round the Sun in slightly less than 365¼ days. It follows that a calendar based upon the Earth's movements round the Sun requires constant adjustment if it is to remain in relation to the seasons of the year, and that a calendar based upon the Moon's changes cannot, without adjustment, be brought into relation with it.

The ancient Semitic Calendars were based upon the movements of the moon, and from them both the Christian and Islamic Calendars ultimately derive. They still both follow the same days of the week.

The ancient Arabian Calendar consisted of twelve lunar months. At irregular intervals, usually every two or three years, there was an additional, thirteenth, month, in order to keep the lunar year in relation to the solar year and the agricultural seasons. This led, however, to considerable confusion, since in fact the resulting years corresponded neither with the solar nor with the lunar system.

The Islamic Calendar is a religious calendar, based upon the Moon's changes. The year consists of twelve lunar months, alternatively of 30 and 29 days. Within each cycle an additional day was added to the last month, Dhu al-Hijja in the 2nd, 5th, 7th, 10th, 13th, 14th, 16th, 19th, 22nd, 24th and 27th years. These are known as *Kabisa* years. In this way an ordinary year consisted of 354 days, and a *Kabisa* year of 355. While conforming to the lunar year, it bore no relation to the solar year.

The essential innovation of Islam was the prohibition of the intercalary months. In the Mishkat, book XI, chapter XI, it is related that the Prophet Muhammad, reciting the *khutbah*, or Sermon, at his Farewell Pilgrimage, said: 'A year is twelve months, as at the time of Creation.' In the Quran, Sura IX, verse 36, it says: 'Verily twelve months is the number of the months with God, according to God's Book, ever since the day when He created Heaven and Earth.' It should be noted that this announcement was made at the end of A H 10 (AD 632), shortly before the Prophet's death. It is therefore not certain that no intercalary months were added in any of the first nine Islamic Years. Thus Christian dates for those years are uncertain.

In AD 622 the Prophet Muhammad was invited by seventy-five inhabitants of Yathrib, now called Medina, to leave Mecca and to make his home with them. After a short delay, two hundred of his followers secretly left Mecca on his instructions. He followed them alone, departing from Mecca on about 10 September AD 622, and arrived at Medina on 24 September AD 622. Seventeen years later the Caliph 'Umar found it necessary to regulate the calendar. He ordered that the lunar year of twelve months should be held to have begun on the first day of the Arabian year in which the Prophet Muhammad left Mecca, 16 July AD 622, and that the Muslim era should be counted from that year. The Prophet Muhammad's departure from Mecca is known in Arabic as the Hijra, or Migration, and the Islamic Calendar is thus known as the era of the Hijra. In English it is usually abbreviated in a Latin form: AH, that is, Anno Hijrae. In this way 16 July AD 622 became officially 1 Muharram AH 1.

As has been said, the Islamic Year is a lunar year which takes no account of the solar year nor of the change of the seasons. Thus, in relation to the solar year, it recedes approximately eleven days each solar year, with the result that in each 32½ years it passes through all the solar seasons. Thus, if in a given lunar year the fasting month of Ramadhan occurs during the heat of the summer, it will occur within the cool season 16¼ years later. It is to be noted that this retrogression of approximately eleven days each year cannot be regarded as precise: according to the actual time of the Moon's changes within the solar year, it is sometimes necessary to reckon it as a change of ten days and on other occasions as one of twelve days.

Although in modern times mathematically calculated Islamic Calendars are printed and widely circulated, it must be emphasized that officially the beginning of each month, and most especially the beginning of the fasting month of Ramadhan, and its end with the first day of the following month Shawwal, depend upon the Moon's changes. Strictly speaking, the new month does not begin until the New Moon has been actually sighted. As to the beginning and end of Ramadhan, while the announcement can in theory be made by any reputable Muslim, the normal observance is that the announcement is made by a Qadi or by some other prominent member of the community. In many places the announcement is made by the firing of a gun, which also marks the opening and close of each day's fasting. The precept of the Quran (Sura II verse 187) is strictly observed: fasting begins when a white thread can be distinguished from a black thread at the dawn of the day.

It frequently happens that the sky is overclouded, and that there is doubt both as to the beginning and end of Ramadhan because the New Moon has not been seen. In this case, as to the beginning of Ramadhan, the normal rule is that Ramadhan is held to begin on the 30th day from the beginning of the preceding month. In these days of modern communication many Muslims listen to the radio to know when Ramadhan has started. In some places, however, the '30th-day rule', is not observed. As to 1 Shawwal, on which the 'Id al-Fitr is celebrated, fasting cannot cease nor the festival begin until the New Moon has been actually seen.

It thus follows that, while the following tables are calculated strictly within terms of these rules, the results cannot be applied with the same strictness. Since the observation of the New Moon is necessary to begin each new month, where there has been cloudy weather, it is quite possible to find, as the writer himself has done, three adjacent villages each claiming a different date as correct, according to the day on which the New Moon had been sighted. It is necessary to make allowances for this in comparing documents, or in hearing evidence in the course of which the witness has given a date according to the Islamic Calendar.

Two

HE CHRISTIAN CALENDAR

❖

The earliest Christians used the calendar devised by Julius Caesar in 46 BC. It was based on the work of Egyptian astronomers. It is known as the Julian Calendar, and still used by the Eastern Orthodox Churches.

The reckoning of years from the Birth of Christ was a change made only in the sixth century AD. Otherwise, with some adjustments, the rules are those established at the First General Council of the Church, held at Nicaea in AD 325. The years are reckoned from the Birth of Christ, and so are known as years AD (Anno Domini: in the year of the Lord). The Calendar follows the solar year of 365¼ days, each common year consisting of 365 days; and each fourth year, or Leap Year, making up the omitted quarters by containing 366 days. The additional day is intercalated on 24 February, the Feast of St Matthias which falls on that day being transferred to the following day, making the month of February consist of 29 days instead of 28 days as in a common year. This system, however, was not precisely in accordance with the solar year, since in fact the additional quarter day is not a complete quarter but only almost so. Thus, in the course of time, the Christian Calendar became in advance of the solar system and out of relation to the seasonal changes and to the agricultural year.

While recognizing the solar year for general purposes, the Council of Nicaea did not recognize it for some religious purposes. The death of Christ on the Cross took place at the Jewish Passover, a festival fixed by the lunar Calendar. It was therefore ordered that the celebration of Good Friday and Easter should take place on the Friday and the Sunday nearest to the Full Moon on which the Passover fell, that is, the Paschal Full Moon. It is for that reason that the cycle of Christian Movable Festivals changes annually in relation to the date on which Easter has fallen. These dates are shown in TABLE EIGHT.

In the year AD 1582 it was realized that the Christian Calendar had reached ten days in advance of the solar year. Thus Pope Gregory XIII ordered that ten days in that year should be omitted from the month of October, and that the fourth day of that month should be followed immediately by the fifteenth day. And, in order to prevent the further accumulation of error, he also ordered that while each year divisible by four should contain 366 days as previously, centenary years whose first two figures are not divisible by four should not be Leap Years. Thus AD 1600 was a Leap Year, but not 1700, 1800 or 1900, while AD 2000 will be a Leap Year. In this way the Christian solar Calendar was once again brought into relation with the lunar Calendar in use for the computation of the date of Easter, which was once again restored to its primitive position as the Sunday nearest to the Full Moon following the Vernal Equinox.

The Christian Calendar as reformed by Pope Gregory XIII was accepted throughout Europe in AD 1582, except in England, Russia and Sweden. The unreformed Calendar is still followed in Russia for ecclesiastical purposes. The reformed Calendar was not adopted in England until 1752, and special information is included in TABLES ONE and FIVE to enable the conversion of Islamic dates to both the unreformed and the reformed Calendar between 1582 and 1752. The reformed Calendar is spoken of as the Gregorian, or New, Style; and the unreformed Calendar as the Julian, or Old, Style.

For England between 1582 and 14 September 1752 see TABLE ONE, pp. 51–56, and TABLE FIVE.

To calculate a date in the Julian Calendar after 1582, ten days should be added up to and including 28 February 1700 in the New Style; then, eleven days until 28 February 1800, twelve days until 28 February 1900, and so on.

The Julian Calendar continues to be used by the Eastern Orthodox Churches in communion with the Orthodox Ecumenical Patriarch of Constantinople. The Armenian, Coptic, Ethiopian and other eastern churches observe variants of the Julian Calendar, their Eras beginning from different base years.

THREE

ETHOD OF USING TABLES ONE TO EIGHT

❖

TABLES ONE to EIGHT enable the conversion of any given Islamic date to the corresponding Christian date, or vice versa, including also the days of the week and the principal festivals of either religion. These tables contain the following information:

TABLE ONE has five columns, and a sixth column between the years AD 1583 and AD 1752 added in brackets. The first column shows the Hijra Year; the second column the Christian date of 1 Muharram, on which the Hijra Year begins; the third column the day on which 1 Muharram fell; the fourth column the number of days which have already elapsed in the Christian Year before that day; and the fifth column the day of the week on which that Christian Year began. The sixth column between the years AD 1583 and AD 1752 shows the day of the week on which the unreformed Christian Year began, as observed during that period in England, Sweden and Russia.

TABLE TWO shows the Islamic months, the first column being the day of the month, and the second the day of the Hijra Year.

TABLE THREE shows the months of the Christian Year: the first column shows the day of the year in both Common and Leap Years, the second column the day of the month in Common Years, and the third column the day of the month in Leap Years. It will be observed that the days of the year as between Common and Leap Years differ only after 28 February.

TABLE FOUR shows the days of the week in the Christian Year arranged as a perpetual calendar according to the day of the week on which that year has begun, for both Common Years and Leap Years, as shown in columns three and five of TABLE ONE.

TABLE FIVE is a separate calendar for the last three months of the year AD 1582.

TABLE SIX is a list of the Principal Islamic Festivals.

TABLE SEVEN shows the Principal Fixed Christian Festivals which are determined by the solar calendar.

TABLE EIGHT shows the Movable Christian Festivals between the years AD 1995 and 2222 as determined by the changes of the date of Easter.

There now follow the six differing methods by which Islamic dates are converted to Christian dates, the method of finding an Islamic date from a Christian date, and the method of employment of the tables for the various festivals. Those using these tables are recommended first to look at the words in small capitals which describe each different method, and to make sure that the correct method is being employed.

1. TO FIND A CHRISTIAN DATE FROM AN ISLAMIC DATE.

Supposing the reader wishes to find the Christian date corresponding to 7 Muharram 1040, he should first take a piece of paper and write this date in full at the top. He should then turn to TABLE ONE, where he will find that the Hijra Year 1040 began on 10 August AD 1630, on which day 221 days of the Christian Year had already elapsed. He will also note that the year AD 1630 began on a Tuesday. Underneath the Islamic date he should therefore write: AH 1040 began 10 August AD 1630 (Tuesday) = 221. He should next turn to TABLE TWO, where it shows that 7 Muharram is the 7th day of the Islamic Year. Thus, underneath the second line of what he has written, he puts: 7 Muharram = 7, being careful to ensure that the figure 7 falls below 221 in the preceding line. He then adds 221+7, the result being 228. He should then look for the 228th day of the Christian Year in TABLE THREE, which shows it to be 16 August. Finally he turns to TABLE FOUR, bearing in mind that AD 1630 was a common year which began on a Tuesday. Thus he finds that 7 Muharram AH 1040 began at sunset on Wednesday, 16 August 1630. The results of his workings will appear as follows:

7 Muharram 1040
AH 1040 began 10 Aug. AD 1630 (Tuesday)   = 221
7 Muharram   =   7

                                                  ———
                                                  228 = 16 Aug. 1630
                                                        Friday

Another example:

16 Jumada al-Ula 1323		
AH 1323 began 8 March AD 1905 (Wednesday)	=	66
16 Jumada al-Ula	=	134
		———
		200 = 19 July 1905
		Wednesday

II. TO FIND A CHRISTIAN DATE FROM AN ISLAMIC DATE WHERE THE CHRISTIAN YEAR IS A LEAP YEAR.

All Leap Years are distinguished in TABLE ONE by the sign † immediately preceding the Christian date corresponding to 1 Muharram. In this case the reader must refer to the third column of TABLE THREE when ascertaining the Christian date, and, in using TABLE FOUR, to use one of the calendars for a Leap Year.

For example:

27 Safar 1351		
AH 1351 began † 7 May AD 1932 (Saturday)	=	127
27 Safar	=	57
		———
		184 = 2 July 1932
		Saturday

III. TO FIND A CHRISTIAN DATE FROM AN ISLAMIC DATE WHERE THE HIJRA YEAR BEGINS IN ONE CHRISTIAN YEAR BUT THE ISLAMIC DATE IS IN THE FOLLOWING CHRISTIAN YEAR.

Most Hijra Years begin in one Christian Year and end in the following Christian Year. If the Islamic date to be converted occurs in the second of the two Christian Years, it is necessary to deduct 365, being the number of days in a common year, from the sum of the days elapsed in the Christian Year and the number of days reached in the Hijra Year.

For example:

2 Shawwal 904	
AH 904 began 19 Aug. AD 1498 (Monday)	= 230
2 Shawwal	= 268
	——
	498
Deduct the number of days in AD 1498:	365
	——
	133 = 13 May 1499
	Monday

In this case care must be taken to ascertain the day on which AD 1499 began, consulting TABLE FOUR accordingly.

Another example:

12 Dhu al-Hijja 1366	
AH 1366 began 25 Nov. AD 1946 (Monday)	= 328
12 Dhu al-Hijja	= 337
	——
	665
Deduct the number of days in AD 1946:	365
	——
	300 = 27 Oct. 1947
	Monday

IV. AS III, BUT WHEN THE FIRST OF THE TWO CHRISTIAN YEARS IS A LEAP YEAR.

In this case it is necessary to deduct 366 days, and not 365, and to use the calendars appropriate to Common Years in TABLE FOUR.

For example:

21 Ramadhan 630
AH 630 began † 18 Oct. AD 1232 (Monday)   =   291
21 Ramadhan   =   257
                                                 ―――
                                                 548
                                                 −366
                                                 ―――
                                                 182   = 1 July 1233
                                                         Saturday

V. AS III, BUT WHEN THE SECOND OF THE TWO CHRISTIAN YEARS IS A LEAP YEAR.

In this case it is necessary to deduct only 365 days, but the third column of TABLE THREE must be used to ascertain the Christian date and also the calendars appropriate to Leap Year in TABLE FOUR.

For example:

1 Shawwal 1202
AH 1202 began on 13 Oct. AD 1787 (Saturday) =   285
1 Shawwal   =   267
                                                ―――
                                                552
                                                −365
                                                ―――
                                                187   = 5 July 1788
                                                        Saturday

vi. To find Christian dates between 15 October 1582 and 14 September 1752 according to the Julian, or Old, Style.

As has been said, England did not adopt the Gregorian, or New Style, until 14 September 1752. By this time the error in her calendar was eleven days, and this was corrected by making 14 September follow immediately upon 2 September in that year. In the present tables, calculation has been based upon the Gregorian Calendar from its inception. If between 15 October 1582 and 14 September 1752 it is wished to calculate in the Julian, or Old, Style ten days should be added to the day of the Christian Year as shown in Table Three between 1 January 1583 and 28 February 1700 inclusive and eleven days between 29 February 1700 and 2 September 1752 inclusive. During this period there was a consequent difference in the days of the week. Thus from 1583 until 1752 the last column of Table One shows in brackets the day of the week on which 1 January fell according to the Old Style. To ascertain the day of the week during 1582 the Old Style follows the calendar for a common year in which 1 January fell on a Saturday. As to the New Style, a separate calendar, showing also the day of the year, is given in Table Five.

vii. To find an Islamic date from a Christian date.

This is done by simply reversing the processes already described. The Christian date should first be written down in full, followed by the day of the year, as ascertained from Table Three. Table One should then be consulted to find out the corresponding Islamic Year. This should be written down together with the number of days shown to have elapsed in the Christian Year on the day on which it began. If the number of days elapsed in the Christian Year on 1 Muharram is less than the number of days of the year on the date concerned, then it should be deducted from the latter.

For example:

1 September AD 1930   =   244
AH 1349 began 29 May AD 1930   =   148
                                                      ———
                                  96 = 7 Rabi' al-Thani AH 1349.

The same method is employed in Leap Years, care having been taken to consult the third column of TABLE THREE to ascertain the day of the Christian Year.

It occurs, however, that inspection of TABLE ONE will show that the relevant Islamic Year began in the preceding Christian Year to that under reference. Thus, for example, the Islamic Year in which 4 September 1946 occurred began in 1945. In this case the number of days reached in the Christian Year is first ascertained and written down. The preceding Islamic Year is then written down with the Christian date on which 1 Muharram fell, followed by the number of days then elapsed in the Christian Year. The latter number is then deducted from the total number of days in the relevant Christian Year, 365 in common years, and 366 in Leap Years. The result is then added to the number of days reached in the Christian Year, this result giving the number of days which has been reached in the Islamic Year. TABLE TWO is then searched for the day of the month corresponding to this result.

For example:

4 September 1946   247
AH 1366 began 6 December AD 1945
339 from 365   =   26
                                                     ———
                                                     273
                                           =   7 Shawwal AH 1366.

VIII. Use of Tables Six to Eight.

Table Six gives the dates of the principal Islamic Festivals, all of which begin on fixed dates. The Christian dates on which they occur can rapidly be found for each year by reference to the preceding tables. It should be remembered that all of these festivals begin at sundown.

Tables Seven and Eight list the principal Christian Fixed and Movable Festivals. In finding the corresponding Islamic dates it is to be recollected that all these festivals begin at midnight and not at sunset.

THE HIJRA YEAR AND THE CHRISTIAN YEAR

TABLE ONE:
The Hijra Year and the Christian Year

Hijra Year	Christian date of 1 Muharram	Day on which 1 Muharram fell	Number of days elapsed in the Christian Year	Day on which the Christian Year began
1	16 July 622	F	196	F
2*	5 July 623	Tu	185	S
3	† 24 June 624	**S**	175	**S**
4	13 June 625	Th	163	Tu
5*	2 June 626	M	152	W
6	23 May 627	S	142	Th
7*	† 11 May 628	W	131	F
8	1 May 629	M	120	**S**
9	20 April 630	F	109	M
10*	9 April 631	Tu	98	Tu
11	† 29 March 632	**S**	88	W
12	18 March 633	Th	76	F
13*	7 March 634	M	65	S
14	25 February 635	S	55	**S**
15	† 14 February 636	W	44	M
16*	2 February 637	**S**	32	W
17	23 January 638	F	22	Th
18*	12 January 639	Tu	11	F
19	† 2 January 640	**S**	1	S
20	† 21 December 640	Th	355	S
21*	10 December 641	M	343	M
22	30 November 642	S	333	Tu
23	19 November 643	W	322	W
24*	† 7 November 644	**S**	311	Th
25	28 October 645	F	300	S
26*	17 October 646	Tu	289	**S**
27	7 October 647	**S**	279	M
28	† 25 September 648	Th	268	Tu
29*	14 September 649	M	256	Th
30	4 September 650	S	246	F

*A Kabisa Year   † A Leap Year

Hijra Year	Christian date of 1 Muharram	Day on which 1 Muharram fell	Number of days elapsed in the Christian Year	Day on which the Christian Year began
31	24 August 651	W	235	S
32*	† 12 August 652	**S**	224	**S**
33	2 August 653	F	213	Tu
34	22 July 654	Tu	202	W
35*	11 July 655	S	191	Th
36	† 30 June 656	Th	181	F
37*	19 June 657	M	169	**S**
38	9 June 658	S	159	M
39	29 May 659	W	148	Tu
40*	† 17 May 660	**S**	137	W
41	7 May 661	F	126	F
42	26 April 662	Tu	115	S
43*	15 April 663	S	104	**S**
44	† 4 April 664	Th	94	M
45	24 March 665	M	82	W
46*	13 March 666	F	71	Th
47	3 March 667	W	61	F
48*	† 20 February 668	**S**	50	S
49	9 February 669	F	39	M
50	29 January 670	Tu	28	Tu
51*	18 January 671	S	17	W
52	† 8 January 672	Th	7	Th
53	† 27 December 672	M	361	Th
54*	16 December 673	F	349	S
55	6 December 674	W	339	**S**
56*	25 November 675	**S**	328	M
57	† 14 November 676	F	318	Tu
58	3 November 677	Tu	306	Th
59*	23 October 678	S	295	F
60	13 October 679	Th	285	S

*A *Kabisa* Year   † A *Leap* Year

Table One:
The Hijra Year and the Christian Year

Hijra Year	Christian date of 1 Muharram	Day on which 1 Muharram fell	Number of days elapsed in the Christian Year	Day on which the Christian Year began
61	† 1 October 680	M	274	**S**
62*	20 September 681	F	262	Tu
63	10 September 682	W	252	W
64	30 August 683	**S**	241	Th
65*	† 18 August 684	Th	230	F
66	8 August 685	Tu	219	**S**
67*	28 July 686	S	208	M
68	18 July 687	Th	198	Tu
69	† 6 July 688	M	187	W
70*	25 June 689	F	175	F
71	15 June 690	W	165	S
72	4 June 691	**S**	154	**S**
73*	† 23 May 692	Th	143	M
74	13 May 693	Tu	132	W
75	2 May 694	S	121	Th
76*	21 April 695	W	110	F
77	† 10 April 696	M	100	S
78*	30 March 697	F	88	M
79	20 March 698	W	78	Tu
80	9 March 699	**S**	67	W
81*	† 26 February 700	Th	56	Th
82	15 February 701	Tu	45	S
83	4 February 702	S	34	**S**
84*	24 January 703	W	23	M
85	† 14 January 704	M	13	Tu
86*	2 January 705	F	1	Th
87	23 December 705	W	356	Th
88	12 December 706	**S**	345	F
89*	1 December 707	Th	334	S
90	† 20 November 708	Tu	324	**S**

*A Kabisa Year   † A Leap Year

20

Hijra Year	Christian date of 1 Muharram	Day on which 1 Muharram fell	Number of days elapsed in the Christian Year	Day on which the Christian Year began
91	9 November 709	S	312	Tu
92*	29 October 710	W	301	W
93	19 October 711	M	291	Th
94	† 7 October 712	F	280	F
95*	26 September 713	Tu	268	**S**
96	16 September 714	**S**	258	M
97*	5 September 715	Th	247	Tu
98	† 25 August 716	Tu	237	W
99	14 August 717	S	225	F
100*	3 August 718	W	214	S
101	24 July 719	M	204	**S**
102*	† 12 July 720	F	193	M
103	1 July 721	Tu	181	W
104	21 June 722	**S**	171	Th
105	10 June 723	Th	160	F
106*	† 29 May 724	M	149	S
107	19 May 725	S	138	M
108*	8 May 726	W	127	Tu
109	28 April 727	M	117	W
110	† 16 April 728	F	106	Th
111*	5 April 729	Tu	94	S
112	26 March 730	**S**	84	**S**
113	15 March 731	Th	73	M
114*	† 3 March 732	M	62	Tu
115	21 February 733	S	51	Th
116*	10 February 734	W	40	F
117	31 January 735	M	30	S
118	† 20 January 736	F	19	**S**
119*	8 January 737	Tu	7	Tu
120	29 December 737	**S**	362	Tu

*A Kabisa Year   † A Leap Year

Hijra Year	Christian date of 1 Muharram	Day on which 1 Muharram fell	Number of days elapsed in the Christian Year	Day on which the Christian Year began
121	18 December 738	Th	351	W
122*	7 December 739	M	340	Th
123	† 26 November 740	S	330	F
124	15 November 741	W	318	**S**
125*	4 November 742	**S**	307	M
126	25 October 743	F	297	Tu
127*	† 13 October 744	Tu	286	W
128	3 October 745	**S**	275	F
129	22 September 746	Th	264	S
130*	11 September 747	M	253	**S**
131	† 31 August 748	S	243	M
132	20 August 749	W	231	W
133*	9 August 750	**S**	220	Th
134	30 July 751	F	210	F
135	† 18 July 752	Tu	199	S
136*	7 July 753	S	187	M
137	27 June 754	Th	177	Tu
138*	16 June 755	M	166	W
139	† 5 June 756	S	156	Th
140	25 May 757	W	144	S
141*	14 May 758	**S**	133	**S**
142	4 May 759	F	123	M
143	† 22 April 760	Tu	112	Tu
144*	11 April 761	S	100	Th
145	1 April 762	Th	90	F
146*	21 March 763	M	79	S
147	† 10 March 764	S	69	**S**
148	27 February 765	W	57	Tu
149*	16 February 766	**S**	46	W
150	6 February 767	F	36	Th

*A *Kabisa* Year   † A *Leap* Year

Hijra Year	Christian date of 1 Muharram	Day on which 1 Muharram fell	Number of days elapsed in the Christian Year	Day on which the Christian Year began
151	† 26 January 768	Tu	25	F
152*	14 January 769	S	13	S
153	4 January 770	Th	3	M
154	24 December 770	M	357	M
155*	13 December 771	F	346	Tu
156	† 2 December 772	W	336	W
157*	21 November 773	S	324	F
158	11 November 774	F	314	S
159	31 October 775	Tu	303	S
160*	† 19 October 776	S	292	M
161	9 October 777	Th	281	W
162	28 September 778	M	270	Th
163*	17 September 779	F	259	F
164	† 6 September 780	W	249	S
165	26 August 781	S	237	M
166*	15 August 782	Th	226	Tu
167	5 August 783	Tu	216	W
168*	† 24 July 784	S	205	Th
169	14 July 785	Th	194	S
170	3 July 786	M	183	S
171*	22 June 787	F	172	M
172	† 11 June 788	W	162	Tu
173	31 May 789	S	150	Th
174*	20 May 790	Th	139	F
175	10 May 791	Tu	129	S
176*	† 28 April 792	S	118	S
177	18 April 793	Th	107	Tu
178	7 April 794	M	96	W
179*	27 March 795	F	85	Th
180	† 16 March 796	W	75	F

*A *Kabisa Year*   † A *Leap Year*

Hijra Year	Christian date of 1 Muharram	Day on which 1 Muharram fell	Number of days elapsed in the Christian Year	Day on which the Christian Year began
181	5 March 797	**S**	63	**S**
182*	22 February 798	Th	52	M
183	12 February 799	Tu	42	Tu
184	† 1 February 800	S	31	W
185*	20 January 801	W	19	F
186	10 January 802	M	9	S
187*	30 December 802	F	363	S
188	20 December 803	W	353	**S**
189	† 8 December 804	**S**	342	M
190*	27 November 805	Th	330	W
191	17 November 806	Tu	320	Th
192	6 November 807	S	309	F
193*	† 25 October 808	W	298	S
194	15 October 809	M	287	M
195	4 October 810	F	276	Tu
196*	23 September 811	Tu	265	W
197	† 12 September 812	**S**	255	Th
198*	1 September 813	Th	243	S
199	22 August 814	Tu	233	**S**
200	11 August 815	S	222	M
201*	† 30 July 816	W	211	Tu
202	20 July 817	M	200	Th
203	9 July 818	F	189	F
204*	28 June 819	Tu	178	S
205	† 17 June 820	**S**	168	**S**
206*	6 June 821	Th	156	Tu
207	27 May 822	Tu	146	W
208	16 May 823	S	135	Th
209*	† 4 May 824	W	124	F
210	24 April 825	M	113	**S**

*A Kabisa Year   † A Leap Year

Hijra Year	Christian date of 1 Muharram	Day on which 1 Muharram fell	Number of days elapsed in the Christian Year	Day on which the Christian Year began
211	13 April 826	F	102	M
212*	2 April 827	Tu	91	Tu
213	† 22 March 828	**S**	81	W
214	11 March 829	Th	69	F
215*	28 February 830	M	58	S
216	18 February 831	S	48	**S**
217*	† 7 February 832	W	37	M
218	27 January 833	M	26	W
219	16 January 834	F	15	Th
220*	5 January 835	Tu	4	F
221	26 December 835	**S**	359	F
222	† 14 December 836	Th	348	S
223*	3 December 837	M	336	M
224	23 November 838	S	326	Tu
225	12 November 839	W	315	W
226*	† 31 October 840	**S**	304	Th
227	21 October 841	F	293	S
228*	10 October 842	Tu	282	**S**
229	30 September 843	**S**	272	M
230	† 18 September 844	Th	261	Tu
231*	7 September 845	M	249	Th
232	28 August 846	S	239	F
233	17 August 847	W	228	S
234*	† 5 August 848	**S**	217	**S**
235	26 July 849	F	206	Tu
236*	15 July 850	Tu	195	W
237	5 July 851	**S**	185	Th
238	† 23 June 852	Th	174	F
239*	12 June 853	M	162	**S**
240	2 June 854	S	152	M

*A Kabisa Year   † A Leap Year

Hijra Year	Christian date of 1 Muharram	Day on which 1 Muharram fell	Number of days elapsed in the Christian Year	Day on which the Christian Year began
241	22 May 855	W	141	Tu
242*	† 10 May 856	**S**	130	W
243	30 April 857	F	119	F
244	19 April 858	Tu	108	S
245*	8 April 859	S	97	**S**
246	† 28 March 860	Th	87	M
247*	17 March 861	M	75	W
248	7 March 862	S	65	Th
249	24 February 863	W	54	F
250*	† 13 February 864	**S**	43	S
251	2 February 865	F	32	M
252	22 January 866	Tu	21	Tu
253*	11 January 867	S	10	W
254	† 1 January 868	Th	0	Th
255	† 20 December 868	M	354	Th
256*	9 December 869	F	342	S
257	29 November 870	W	332	**S**
258*	18 November 871	**S**	321	M
259	† 7 November 872	F	311	Tu
260	27 October 873	Tu	299	Th
261*	16 October 874	S	288	F
262	6 October 875	Th	278	S
263	† 24 September 876	M	267	**S**
264*	13 September 877	F	255	Tu
265	3 September 878	W	245	W
266*	23 August 879	**S**	234	Th
267	† 12 August 880	F	224	F
268	1 August 881	Tu	212	**S**
269*	21 July 882	S	201	M
270	11 July 883	Th	191	Tu

*A *Kabisa Year*   † A *Leap Year*

Hijra Year	Christian date of 1 Muharram	Day on which 1 Muharram fell	Number of days elapsed in the Christian Year	Day on which the Christian Year began
271	† 29 June 884	M	180	W
272*	18 June 885	F	168	F
273	8 June 886	W	158	S
274	28 May 887	**S**	147	**S**
275*	† 16 May 888	Th	136	M
276	6 May 889	Tu	125	W
277*	25 April 890	S	114	Th
278	15 April 891	Th	104	F
279	† 3 April 892	M	93	S
280*	23 March 893	F	81	M
281	13 March 894	W	71	Tu
282	2 March 895	**S**	60	W
283*	† 19 February 896	Th	49	Th
284	8 February 897	Tu	38	S
285	28 January 898	S	27	**S**
286*	17 January 899	W	16	M
287	† 7 January 900	M	6	Tu
288*	† 26 December 900	F	360	Tu
289	16 December 901	W	349	Th
290	5 December 902	**S**	338	F
291*	24 November 903	Th	327	S
292	† 13 November 904	Tu	317	**S**
293	2 November 905	S	305	Tu
294*	22 October 906	W	294	W
295	12 October 907	M	284	Th
296*	† 30 September 908	F	273	F
297	20 September 909	W	262	**S**
298	9 September 910	**S**	251	M
299*	29 August 911	Th	240	Tu
300	† 18 August 912	Tu	230	W

*A Kabisa Year   † A Leap Year

Hijra Year	Christian date of 1 Muharram	Day on which 1 Muharram fell	Number of days elapsed in the Christian Year	Day on which the Christian Year began
301	7 August 913	S	218	F
302*	27 July 914	W	207	S
303	17 July 915	M	197	**S**
304	† 5 July 916	F	186	M
305*	24 June 917	Tu	174	W
306	14 June 918	**S**	164	Th
307*	3 June 919	Th	153	F
308	† 23 May 920	Tu	143	S
309	12 May 921	S	131	M
310*	1 May 922	W	120	Tu
311	21 April 923	M	110	W
312	† 9 April 924	F	99	Th
313*	29 March 925	Tu	87	S
314	19 March 926	**S**	77	**S**
315	8 March 927	Th	66	M
316*	† 25 February 928	M	55	Tu
317	14 February 929	S	44	Th
318*	3 February 930	W	33	F
319	24 January 931	M	23	S
320	† 13 January 932	F	12	**S**
321*	1 January 933	Tu	0	Tu
322	22 December 933	**S**	355	Tu
323	11 December 934	Th	344	W
324*	30 November 935	M	333	Th
325	† 19 November 936	S	323	F
326*	8 November 937	W	311	**S**
327	29 October 938	M	301	M
328	18 October 939	F	290	Tu
329*	† 6 October 940	Tu	279	W
330	26 September 941	**S**	268	F

*A Kabisa Year   † A Leap Year

Hijra Year	Christian date of 1 Muharram	Day on which 1 Muharram fell	Number of days elapsed in the Christian Year	Day on which the Christian Year began
331	15 September 942	Th	257	S
332*	4 September 943	M	246	**S**
333	† 24 August 944	S	236	M
334	13 August 945	W	224	W
335*	2 August 946	**S**	213	Th
336	23 July 947	F	203	F
337*	† 11 July 948	Tu	192	S
338	1 July 949	**S**	181	M
339	20 June 950	Th	170	Tu
340*	9 June 951	M	159	W
341	† 29 May 952	S	149	Th
342	18 May 953	W	137	S
343*	7 May 954	**S**	126	**S**
344	27 April 955	F	116	M
345	† 15 April 956	Tu	105	Tu
346*	4 April 957	S	93	Th
347	25 March 958	Th	83	F
348*	14 March 959	M	72	S
349	† 3 March 960	S	62	**S**
350	20 February 961	W	50	Tu
351*	9 February 962	**S**	39	W
352	30 January 963	F	29	Th
353	† 19 January 964	Tu	18	F
354*	7 January 965	S	6	**S**
355	28 December 965	Th	361	**S**
356*	17 December 966	M	350	M
357	7 December 967	S	340	Tu
358	† 25 November 968	W	329	W
359*	14 November 969	**S**	317	F
360	4 November 970	F	307	S

*A Kabisa Year   † A Leap Year

Hijra Year	Christian date of 1 Muharram	Day on which 1 Muharram fell	Number of days elapsed in the Christian Year	Day on which the Christian Year began
361	24 October 971	Tu	296	**S**
362*	† 12 October 972	S	285	M
363	2 October 973	Th	274	W
364	21 September 974	M	263	Th
365*	10 September 975	F	252	F
366	† 30 August 976	W	242	S
367*	19 August 977	**S**	230	M
368	9 August 978	F	220	Tu
369	29 July 979	Tu	209	W
370*	† 17 July 980	S	198	Th
371	7 July 981	Th	187	S
372	26 June 982	M	176	**S**
373*	15 June 983	F	165	M
374	† 4 June 984	W	155	Tu
375	24 May 985	**S**	143	Th
376*	13 May 986	Th	132	F
377	3 May 987	Tu	122	S
378*	† 21 April 988	S	111	**S**
379	11 April 989	Th	100	Tu
380	31 March 990	M	89	W
381*	20 March 991	F	78	Th
382	† 9 March 992	W	68	F
383	26 February 993	**S**	56	**S**
384*	15 February 994	Th	45	M
385	5 February 995	Tu	35	Tu
386*	† 25 January 996	S	24	W
387	14 January 997	Th	13	F
388	3 January 998	M	2	S
389*	23 December 998	F	356	S
390	13 December 999	W	346	**S**

*A *Kabisa* Year   † A *Leap* Year

TABLE ONE:
THE HIJRA YEAR AND THE CHRISTIAN YEAR

Hijra Year	Christian date of 1 Muharram	Day on which 1 Muharram fell	Number of days elapsed in the Christian Year	Day on which the Christian Year began
391	† 1 December 1000	**S**	335	M
392*	20 November 1001	Th	323	W
393	10 November 1002	Tu	313	Th
394	30 October 1003	S	302	F
395*	† 18 October 1004	W	291	S
396	8 October 1005	M	280	M
397*	27 September 1006	F	269	Tu
398	17 September 1007	W	259	W
399	† 5 September 1008	**S**	248	Th
400*	25 August 1009	Th	236	S
401	15 August 1010	Tu	226	**S**
402	4 August 1011	S	215	M
403*	† 23 July 1012	W	204	Tu
404	13 July 1013	M	193	Th
405	2 July 1014	F	182	F
406*	21 June 1015	Tu	171	S
407	† 10 June 1016	**S**	161	**S**
408*	30 May 1017	Th	149	Tu
409	20 May 1018	Tu	139	W
410	9 May 1019	S	128	Th
411*	† 27 April 1020	W	117	F
412	17 April 1021	M	106	**S**
413	6 April 1022	F	95	M
414*	26 March 1023	Tu	84	Tu
415	† 15 March 1024	**S**	74	W
416*	4 March 1025	Th	62	F
417	22 February 1026	Tu	52	S
418	11 February 1027	S	41	**S**
419*	† 31 January 1028	W	30	M
420	20 January 1029	M	19	W

*A Kabisa Year   † A Leap Year

Hijra Year	Christian date of 1 Muharram	Day on which 1 Muharram fell	Number of days elapsed in the Christian Year	Day on which the Christian Year began
421	9 January 1030	F	8	Th
422*	29 December 1030	Tu	362	Th
423	19 December 1031	S	352	F
424	† 7 December 1032	Th	341	S
425*	26 November 1033	M	329	M
426	16 November 1034	S	319	Tu
427*	5 November 1035	W	308	W
428	† 25 October 1036	M	298	Th
429	14 October 1037	F	286	S
430*	3 October 1038	Tu	275	S
431	23 September 1039	S	265	M
432	† 11 September 1040	Th	254	Tu
433*	31 August 1041	M	242	Th
434	21 August 1042	S	232	F
435	10 August 1043	W	221	S
436*	† 29 July 1044	S	210	S
437	19 July 1045	F	199	Tu
438*	8 July 1046	Tu	188	W
439	28 June 1047	S	178	Th
440	† 16 June 1048	Th	167	F
441*	5 June 1049	M	155	S
442	26 May 1050	S	145	M
443	15 May 1051	W	134	Tu
444*	† 3 May 1052	S	123	W
445	23 April 1053	F	112	F
446*	12 April 1054	Tu	101	S
447	2 April 1055	S	91	S
448	† 21 March 1056	Th	80	M
449*	10 March 1057	M	68	W
450	28 February 1058	S	58	Th

*A Kabisa Year   † A Leap Year

Hijra Year	Christian date of 1 Muharram	Day on which 1 Muharram fell	Number of days elapsed in the Christian Year	Day on which the Christian Year began
451	17 February 1059	W	47	F
452*	† 6 February 1060	**S**	36	S
453	26 January 1061	F	25	M
454	15 January 1062	Tu	14	Tu
455*	4 January 1063	S	3	W
456	25 December 1063	Th	358	W
457*	† 13 December 1064	M	347	Th
458	3 December 1065	S	336	S
459	22 November 1066	W	325	**S**
460*	11 November 1067	**S**	314	M
461	† 31 October 1068	F	304	Tu
462	20 October 1069	Tu	292	Th
463*	9 October 1070	S	281	F
464	29 September 1071	Th	271	S
465	† 17 September 1072	M	260	**S**
466*	6 September 1073	F	248	Tu
467	27 August 1074	W	238	W
468*	16 August 1075	**S**	227	Th
469	† 5 August 1076	F	217	F
470	25 July 1077	Tu	205	**S**
471*	14 July 1078	S	194	M
472	4 July 1079	Th	184	Tu
473	† 22 June 1080	M	173	W
474*	11 June 1081	F	161	F
475	1 June 1082	W	151	S
476*	21 May 1083	**S**	140	**S**
477	† 10 May 1084	F	130	M
478	29 April 1085	Tu	118	W
479*	18 April 1086	S	107	Th
480	8 April 1087	Th	97	F

*A *Kabisa Year*   † A *Leap Year*

Hijra Year	Christian date of 1 Muharram	Day on which 1 Muharram fell	Number of days elapsed in the Christian Year	Day on which the Christian Year began
481	† 27 March 1088	M	86	S
482*	16 March 1089	F	74	M
483	6 March 1090	W	64	Tu
484	23 February 1091	**S**	53	W
485*	† 12 February 1092	Th	42	Th
486	1 February 1093	Tu	31	S
487*	21 January 1094	S	20	**S**
488	11 January 1095	Th	10	M
489	31 December 1095	M	364	M
490*	† 19 December 1096	F	353	Tu
491	9 December 1097	W	342	Th
492	28 November 1098	**S**	331	F
493*	17 November 1099	Th	320	S
494	† 6 November 1100	Tu	310	**S**
495	26 October 1101	S	298	Tu
496*	15 October 1102	W	287	W
497	5 October 1103	M	277	Th
498*	† 23 September 1104	F	266	F
499	13 September 1105	W	255	**S**
500	2 September 1106	**S**	244	M
501*	22 August 1107	Th	233	Tu
502	† 11 August 1108	Tu	223	W
503	31 July 1109	S	211	F
504*	20 July 1110	W	200	S
505	10 July 1111	M	190	**S**
506*	† 28 June 1112	F	179	M
507	18 June 1113	W	168	W
508	7 June 1114	**S**	157	Th
509*	27 May 1115	Th	146	F
510	† 16 May 1116	Tu	136	S

*A *Kabisa* Year   † A *Leap Year*

Hijra Year	Christian date of 1 Muharram	Day on which 1 Muharram fell	Number of days elapsed in the Christian Year	Day on which the Christian Year began
511	5 May 1117	S	124	M
512*	24 April 1118	W	113	Tu
513	14 April 1119	M	103	W
514	† 2 April 1120	F	92	Th
515*	22 March 1121	Tu	80	S
516	12 March 1122	**S**	70	**S**
517*	1 March 1123	Th	59	M
518	† 19 February 1124	Tu	49	Tu
519	7 February 1125	S	37	Th
520*	27 January 1126	W	26	F
521	17 January 1127	M	16	S
522	† 6 January 1128	F	5	**S**
523*	† 25 December 1128	Tu	359	**S**
524	15 December 1129	**S**	348	Tu
525	4 December 1130	Th	337	W
526*	23 November 1131	M	326	Th
527	† 12 November 1132	S	316	F
528*	1 November 1133	W	304	**S**
529	22 October 1134	M	294	M
530	11 October 1135	F	283	Tu
531*	† 29 September 1136	Tu	272	W
532	19 September 1137	**S**	261	F
533	8 September 1138	Th	250	S
534*	28 August 1139	M	239	**S**
535	† 17 August 1140	S	229	M
536*	6 August 1141	W	217	W
537	27 July 1142	M	207	Th
538	16 July 1143	F	196	F
539*	† 4 July 1144	Tu	185	S
540	24 June 1145	**S**	174	M

*A *Kabisa Year*   † A *Leap Year*

Hijra Year	Christian date of 1 Muharram	Day on which 1 Muharram fell	Number of days elapsed in the Christian Year	Day on which the Christian Year began
541	13 June 1146	Th	163	Tu
542*	2 June 1147	M	152	W
543	† 22 May 1148	S	142	Th
544	11 May 1149	W	130	S
545*	30 April 1150	**S**	119	**S**
546	20 April 1151	F	109	M
547*	† 8 April 1152	Tu	98	Tu
548	29 March 1153	**S**	87	Th
549	18 March 1154	Th	76	F
550*	7 March 1155	M	65	S
551	† 25 February 1156	S	55	**S**
552	13 February 1157	W	43	Tu
553*	2 February 1158	**S**	32	W
554	23 January 1159	F	22	Th
555	† 12 January 1160	Tu	11	F
556*	† 31 December 1160	S	365	F
557	21 December 1161	Th	354	**S**
558*	10 December 1162	M	343	M
559	30 November 1163	S	333	Tu
560	† 18 November 1164	W	322	W
561*	7 November 1165	**S**	310	F
562	28 October 1166	F	300	S
563	17 October 1167	Tu	289	**S**
564*	† 5 October 1168	S	278	M
565	25 September 1169	Th	267	W
566*	14 September 1170	M	256	Th
567	4 September 1171	S	246	F
568	† 23 August 1172	W	235	S
569*	12 August 1173	**S**	223	M
570	2 August 1174	F	213	Tu

*A Kabisa Year   † A Leap Year

Hijra Year	Christian date of 1 Muharram	Day on which 1 Muharram fell	Number of days elapsed in the Christian Year	Day on which the Christian Year began
571	22 July 1175	Tu	202	W
572*	† 10 July 1176	S	191	Th
573	30 June 1177	Th	180	S
574	19 June 1178	M	169	S
575*	8 June 1179	F	158	M
576	† 28 May 1180	W	148	Tu
577*	17 May 1181	S	136	Th
578	7 May 1182	F	126	F
579	26 April 1183	Tu	115	S
580*	† 14 April 1184	S	104	S
581	4 April 1185	Th	93	Tu
582	24 March 1186	M	82	W
583*	13 March 1187	F	71	Th
584	† 2 March 1188	W	61	F
585	19 February 1189	S	49	S
586*	8 February 1190	Th	38	M
587	29 January 1191	Tu	28	Tu
588*	† 18 January 1192	S	17	W
589	7 January 1193	Th	6	F
590	27 December 1193	M	360	F
591*	16 December 1194	F	349	S
592	6 December 1195	W	339	S
593	† 24 November 1196	S	328	M
594*	13 November 1197	Th	316	W
595	3 November 1198	Tu	306	Th
596*	23 October 1199	S	295	F
597	† 12 October 1200	Th	285	S
598	1 October 1201	M	273	M
599*	20 September 1202	F	262	Tu
600	10 September 1203	W	252	W

*A Kabisa Year   † A Leap Year

Hijra Year	Christian date of 1 Muharram	Day on which 1 Muharram fell	Number of days elapsed in the Christian Year	Day on which the Christian Year began
601	† 29 August 1204	**S**	241	Th
602*	18 Augusr 1205	Th	229	S
603	8 August 1206	Tu	219	**S**
604	28 July 1207	S	208	M
605*	† 16 July 1208	W	197	Tu
606	6 July 1209	M	186	Th
607*	25 June 1210	F	175	F
608	15 June 1211	W	165	S
609	† 3 June 1212	**S**	154	**S**
610*	23 May 1213	Th	142	Tu
611	13 May 1214	Tu	132	W
612	2 May 1215	S	121	Th
613*	† 20 April 1216	W	110	F
614	10 April 1217	M	99	**S**
615	30 March 1218	F	88	M
616*	19 March 1219	Tu	77	Tu
617	† 8 March 1220	**S**	67	W
618*	25 February 1221	Th	55	F
619	15 February 1222	Tu	45	S
620	4 February 1223	S	34	**S**
621*	† 24 January 1224	W	23	M
622	13 January 1225	M	12	W
623	2 January 1226	F	1	Th
624*	22 December 1226	Tu	355	Th
625	12 December 1227	**S**	345	F
626*	† 30 November 1228	Th	334	S
627	20 November 1229	Tu	323	M
628	9 November 1230	S	312	Tu
629*	29 October 1231	W	301	W
630	† 18 October 1232	M	291	Th

*A *Kabisa Year*   † A *Leap Year*

Hijra Year	Christian date of 1 Muharram	Day on which 1 Muharram fell	Number of days elapsed in the Christian Year	Day on which the Christian Year began
631	7 October 1233	F	279	S
632*	26 September 1234	Tu	268	**S**
633	16 September 1235	**S**	258	M
634	† 4 September 1236	Th	247	Tu
635*	24 August 1237	M	235	Th
636	14 August 1238	S	225	F
637*	3 August 1239	W	214	S
638	† 23 July 1240	M	204	**S**
639	12 July 1241	F	192	Tu
640*	1 July 1242	Tu	181	W
641	21 June 1243	**S**	171	Th
642	† 9 June 1244	Th	160	F
643*	29 May 1245	M	148	**S**
644	19 May 1246	S	138	M
645	8 May 1247	W	127	Tu
646*	† 26 April 1248	**S**	116	W
647	16 April 1249	F	105	F
648*	5 April 1250	Tu	94	S
649	26 March 1251	**S**	84	**S**
650	† 14 March 1252	Th	73	M
651*	3 March 1253	M	61	W
652	21 February 1254	S	51	Th
653	10 February 1255	W	40	F
654*	† 30 January 1256	**S**	29	S
655	19 January 1257	F	18	M
656*	8 January 1258	Tu	7	Tu
657	29 December 1258	**S**	362	Tu
658	18 December 1259	Th	351	W
659*	† 6 December 1260	M	340	Th
660	26 November 1261	S	329	S

*A Kabisa Year   † A Leap Year

Hijra Year	Christian date of 1 Muharram	Day on which 1 Muharram fell	Number of days elapsed in the Christian Year	Day on which the Christian Year began
661	15 November 1262	W	318	**S**
662*	4 November 1263	**S**	307	M
663	† 24 October 1264	F	297	Tu
664	13 October 1265	Tu	285	Th
665*	2 October 1266	S	274	F
666	22 September 1267	Th	264	S
667*	† 10 September 1268	M	253	**S**
668	31 August 1269	S	242	Tu
669	20 August 1270	W	231	W
670*	9 August 1271	**S**	220	Th
671	† 29 July 1272	F	210	F
672	18 July 1273	Tu	198	**S**
673*	7 July 1274	S	187	M
674	27 June 1275	Th	177	Tu
675	† 15 June 1276	M	166	W
676*	4 June 1277	F	154	F
677	25 May 1278	W	144	S
678*	14 May 1279	**S**	133	**S**
679	† 3 May 1280	F	123	M
680	22 April 1281	Tu	111	W
681*	11 April 1282	S	100	Th
682	1 April 1283	Th	90	F
683	† 20 March 1284	M	79	S
684*	9 March 1285	F	67	M
685	27 February 1286	W	57	Tu
686*	16 February 1287	**S**	46	W
687	† 6 February 1288	F	36	Th
688	25 January 1289	Tu	24	S
689*	14 January 1290	S	13	**S**
690	4 January 1291	Th	3	M

*A *Kabisa Year*   † A *Leap Year*

Hijra Year	Christian date of 1 Muharram	Day on which 1 Muharram fell	Number of days elapsed in the Christian Year	Day on which the Christian Year began
691	24 December 1291	M	357	M
692*	† 12 December 1292	F	346	Tu
693	2 December 1293	W	335	Th
694	21 November 1294	**S**	324	F
695*	10 November 1295	Th	313	S
696	† 30 October 1296	Tu	303	**S**
697*	19 October 1297	S	291	Tu
698	9 October 1298	Th	281	W
699	28 September 1299	M	270	Th
700*	† 16 September 1300	F	259	F
701	6 September 1301	W	248	**S**
702	26 August 1302	**S**	237	M
703*	15 August 1303	Th	226	Tu
704	† 4 August 1304	Tu	216	W
705	24 July 1305	S	204	F
706*	13 July 1306	W	193	S
707	3 July 1307	M	183	**S**
708*	† 21 June 1308	F	172	M
709	11 June 1309	W	161	W
710	31 May 1310	**S**	150	Th
711*	20 May 1311	Th	139	F
712	† 9 May 1312	Tu	129	S
713	28 April 1313	S	117	M
714*	17 April 1314	W	106	Tu
715	7 April 1315	M	96	W
716*	† 26 March 1316	F	85	Th
717	16 March 1317	W	74	S
718	5 March 1318	**S**	63	**S**
719*	22 February 1319	Th	52	M
720	† 12 February 1320	Tu	42	Tu

*A Kabisa Year   † A Leap Year

Hijra Year	Christian date of 1 Muharram	Day on which 1 Muharram fell	Number of days elapsed in the Christian Year	Day on which the Christian Year began
721	31 January 1321	S	30	Th
722*	20 January 1322	W	19	F
723	10 January 1323	M	9	S
724	30 December 1323	F	363	S
725*	† 18 December 1324	Tu	352	**S**
726	8 December 1325	**S**	341	Tu
727*	27 November 1326	Th	330	W
728	17 November 1327	Tu	320	Th
729	† 5 November 1328	S	309	F
730*	25 October 1329	W	297	**S**
731	15 October 1330	M	287	M
732	4 October 1331	F	276	Tu
733*	† 22 September 1332	Tu	265	W
734	12 September 1333	**S**	254	F
735	1 September 1334	Th	243	S
736*	21 August 1335	M	232	**S**
737	† 10 August 1336	S	222	M
738*	30 July 1337	W	210	W
739	20 July 1338	M	200	Th
740	9 July 1339	F	189	F
741*	† 27 June 1340	Tu	178	S
742	17 June 1341	**S**	167	M
743	6 June 1342	Th	156	Tu
744*	26 May 1343	M	145	W
745	† 15 May 1344	S	135	Th
746*	4 May 1345	W	123	S
747	24 April 1346	M	113	**S**
748	13 April 1347	F	102	M
749*	† 1 April 1348	Tu	91	Tu
750	22 March 1349	**S**	80	Th

*A Kabisa Year   † A Leap Year

TABLE ONE:
THE HIJRA YEAR AND THE CHRISTIAN YEAR

Hijra Year	Christian date of 1 Muharram	Day on which 1 Muharram fell	Number of days elapsed in the Christian Year	Day on which the Christian Year began
751	11 March 1350	Th	69	F
752*	28 February 1351	M	58	S
753	† 18 February 1352	S	48	**S**
754	6 February 1353	W	36	Tu
755*	26 January 1354	**S**	25	W
756	16 January 1355	F	15	Th
757*	† 5 January 1356	Tu	4	F
758	† 25 December 1356	**S**	359	F
759	14 December 1357	Th	347	**S**
760*	3 December 1358	M	336	M
761	23 November 1359	S	326	Tu
762	† 11 November 1360	W	315	W
763*	31 October 1361	**S**	303	F
764	21 October 1362	F	293	S
765	10 October 1363	Tu	282	**S**
766*	† 28 September 1364	S	271	M
767	18 September 1365	Th	260	W
768*	7 September 1366	M	249	Th
769	28 August 1367	S	239	F
770	† 16 August 1368	W	228	S
771*	5 August 1369	**S**	216	M
772	26 July 1370	F	206	Tu
773	15 July 1371	Tu	195	W
774*	† 3 July 1372	S	184	Th
775	23 June 1373	Th	173	S
776*	12 June 1374	M	162	**S**
777	2 June 1375	S	152	M
778	† 21 May 1376	W	141	Tu
779*	10 May 1377	**S**	129	Th
780	30 April 1378	F	119	F

*A Kabisa Year   † A Leap Year

Hijra Year	Christian date of 1 Muharram	Day on which 1 Muharram fell	Number of days elapsed in the Christian Year	Day on which the Christian Year began
781	19 April 1379	Tu	108	S
782*	† 7 April 1380	S	97	**S**
783	28 March 1381	Th	86	Tu
784	17 March 1382	M	75	W
785*	6 March 1383	F	64	Th
786	† 24 February 1384	W	54	F
787*	12 February 1385	**S**	42	**S**
788	2 February 1386	F	32	M
789	22 January 1387	Tu	21	Tu
790*	† 11 January 1388	S	10	W
791	† 31 December 1388	Th	365	W
792	20 December 1389	M	353	F
793*	9 December 1390	F	342	S
794	29 November 1391	W	332	**S**
795	† 17 November 1392	**S**	321	M
796*	6 November 1393	Th	309	W
797	27 October 1394	Tu	299	Th
798*	16 October 1395	S	288	F
799	† 5 October 1396	Th	278	S
800	24 September 1397	M	266	M
801*	13 September 1398	F	255	Tu
802	3 September 1399	W	245	W
803	† 22 August 1400	**S**	234	Th
804*	11 August 1401	Th	222	S
805	1 August 1402	Tu	212	**S**
806*	21 July 1403	S	201	M
807	† 10 July 1404	Th	191	Tu
808	29 June 1405	M	179	Th
809*	18 June 1406	F	168	F
810	8 June 1407	W	158	S

*A *Kabisa* Year † A *Leap* Year

Hijra Year	Christian date of 1 Muharram	Day on which 1 Muharram fell	Number of days elapsed in the Christian Year	Day on which the Christian Year began
811	† 27 May 1408	**S**	147	**S**
812*	16 May 1409	Th	135	Tu
813	6 May 1410	Tu	125	W
814	25 April 1411	S	114	Th
815*	† 13 April 1412	W	103	F
816	3 April 1413	M	92	**S**
817*	23 March 1414	F	81	M
818	13 March 1415	W	71	Tu
819	† 1 March 1416	**S**	60	W
820*	18 February 1417	Th	48	F
821	8 February 1418	Tu	38	S
822	28 January 1419	S	27	**S**
823*	† 17 January 1420	W	16	M
824	6 January 1421	M	5	W
825	26 December 1421	F	359	W
826*	15 December 1422	Tu	348	Th
827	5 December 1423	**S**	338	F
828*	† 23 November 1424	Th	327	S
829	13 November 1425	Tu	316	M
830	2 November 1426	S	305	Tu
831*	22 October 1427	W	294	W
832	† 11 October 1428	M	284	Th
833	30 September 1429	F	272	S
834*	19 September 1430	Tu	261	**S**
835	9 September 1431	**S**	251	M
836*	† 28 August 1432	Th	240	Tu
837	18 August 1433	Tu	229	Th
838	7 August 1434	S	218	F
839*	27 July 1435	W	207	S
840	† 16 July 1436	M	197	**S**

*A *Kabisa* Year   † A *Leap* Year

45

Hijra Year	Christian date of 1 Muharram	Day on which 1 Muharram fell	Number of days elapsed in the Christian Year	Day on which the Christian Year began
841	5 July 1437	F	185	Tu
842*	24 June 1438	Tu	174	W
843	14 June 1439	S	164	Th
844	† 2 June 1440	Th	153	F
845*	22 May 1441	M	141	S
846	12 May 1442	S	131	M
847*	1 May 1443	W	120	Tu
848	† 20 April 1444	M	110	W
849	9 April 1445	F	98	F
850*	29 March 1446	Tu	87	S
851	19 March 1447	S	77	S
852	† 7 March 1448	Th	66	M
853*	24 February 1449	M	54	W
854	14 February 1450	S	44	Th
855	3 February 1451	W	33	F
856*	† 23 January 1452	S	22	S
857	12 January 1453	F	11	M
858*	1 January 1454	Tu	0	Tu
859	22 December 1454	S	355	Tu
860	11 December 1455	Th	344	W
861*	† 29 November 1456	M	333	Th
862	19 November 1457	S	322	S
863	8 November 1458	W	311	S
864*	28 October 1459	S	300	M
865	† 17 October 1460	F	290	Tu
866*	6 October 1461	Tu	278	Th
867	26 September 1462	S	268	F
868	15 September 1463	Th	257	S
869*	† 3 September 1464	Tu	246	S
870	24 August 1465	S	235	Tu

*A *Kabisa* Year   † A *Leap* Year

Hijra Year	Christian date of 1 Muharram	Day on which 1 Muharram fell	Number of days elapsed in the Christian Year	Day on which the Christian Year began
871	13 August 1466	W	224	W
872*	2 August 1467	**S**	213	Th
873	† 22 July 1468	F	203	F
874	11 July 1469	Tu	191	**S**
875*	30 June 1470	S	180	M
876	20 June 1471	Th	170	Tu
877*	† 8 June 1472	M	159	W
878	29 May 1473	S	148	F
879	18 May 1474	W	137	S
880*	7 May 1475	**S**	126	**S**
881	† 26 April 1476	F	116	M
882	15 April 1477	Tu	104	W
883*	4 April 1478	S	93	Th
884	25 March 1479	Th	83	F
885	† 13 March 1480	M	72	S
886*	2 March 1481	F	60	M
887	20 February 1482	W	50	Tu
888*	9 February 1483	**S**	39	W
889	† 30 January 1484	F	29	Th
890	18 January 1485	Tu	17	S
891*	7 January 1486	S	6	**S**
892	28 December 1486	Th	361	**S**
893	17 December 1487	M	350	M
894*	† 5 December 1488	F	339	Tu
895	25 November 1489	W	328	Th
896*	14 November 1490	**S**	317	F
897	4 November 1491	F	307	S
898	† 23 October 1492	Tu	296	**S**
899*	12 October 1493	S	284	Tu
900	2 October 1494	Th	274	W

*A *Kabisa* Year   † A *Leap* Year

Hijra Year	Christian date of 1 Muharram	Day on which 1 Muharram fell	Number of days elapsed in the Christian Year	Day on which the Christian Year began
901	21 September 1495	M	263	Th
902*	† 9 September 1496	F	252	F
903	30 August 1497	W	241	S
904	19 August 1498	S	230	M
905*	8 August 1499	Th	219	Tu
906	† 28 July 1500	Tu	209	W
907*	17 July 1501	S	197	F
908	7 July 1502	Th	187	S
909	26 June 1503	M	176	S
910*	† 14 June 1504	F	165	M
911	4 June 1505	W	154	W
912	24 May 1506	S	143	Th
913*	13 May 1507	Th	132	F
914	† 2 May 1508	Tu	122	S
915	21 April 1509	S	110	M
916*	10 April 1510	W	99	Tu
917	31 March 1511	M	89	W
918*	† 19 March 1512	F	78	Th
919	9 March 1513	W	67	S
920	26 February 1514	S	56	S
921*	15 February 1515	Th	45	M
922	† 5 February 1516	Tu	35	Tu
923	24 January 1517	S	23	Th
924*	13 January 1518	W	12	F
925	3 January 1519	M	2	S
926*	23 December 1519	F	356	S
927	† 12 December 1520	W	346	S
928	1 December 1521	S	334	Tu
929*	20 November 1522	Th	323	W
930	10 November 1523	Tu	313	Th

*A *Kabisa Year* † *A Leap Year*

Hijra Year	Christian date of 1 Muharram	Day on which 1 Muharram fell	Number of days elapsed in the Christian Year	Day on which the Christian Year began
931	† 29 October 1524	S	302	F
932*	18 October 1525	W	290	S
933	8 October 1526	M	280	M
934	27 September 1527	F	269	Tu
935*	† 15 September 1528	Tu	258	W
936	5 September 1529	S	247	F
937*	25 August 1530	Th	236	S
938	15 August 1531	Tu	226	S
939	† 3 August 1532	S	215	M
940*	23 July 1533	W	203	W
941	13 July 1534	M	193	Th
942	2 July 1535	F	182	F
943*	† 20 June 1536	Tu	171	S
944	10 June 1537	S	160	M
945	30 May 1538	Th	149	Tu
946*	19 May 1539	M	138	W
947	† 8 May 1540	S	128	Th
948*	27 April 1541	W	116	S
949	17 April 1542	M	106	S
950	6 April 1543	F	95	M
951*	† 25 March 1544	Tu	84	Tu
952	15 March 1545	S	73	Th
953	4 March 1546	Th	62	F
954*	21 February 1547	M	51	S
955	† 11 February 1548	S	41	S
956*	30 January 1549	W	29	Tu
957	20 January 1550	M	19	W
958	9 January 1551	F	8	Th
959*	29 December 1551	Tu	362	Th
960	† 18 December 1552	S	352	F

*A *Kabisa Year*   † A *Leap Year*

Hijra Year	Christian date of 1 Muharram	Day on which 1 Muharram fell	Number of days elapsed in the Christian Year	Day on which the Christian Year began
961	7 December 1553	Th	340	**S**
962*	26 November 1554	M	329	M
963	16 November 1555	S	319	Tu
964	† 4 November 1556	W	308	W
965*	24 October 1557	**S**	296	F
966	14 October 1558	F	286	S
967*	3 October 1559	Tu	275	**S**
968	† 22 September 1560	**S**	265	M
969	11 September 1561	Th	253	W
970*	31 August 1562	M	242	Th
971	21 August 1563	S	232	F
972	† 9 August 1564	W	221	S
973*	29 July 1565	**S**	209	M
974	19 July 1566	F	199	Tu
975	8 July 1567	Tu	188	W
976*	† 26 June 1568	S	177	Th
977	16 June 1569	Th	166	S
978*	5 June 1570	M	155	**S**
979	26 May 1571	S	145	M
980	† 14 May 1572	W	134	Tu
981*	3 May 1573	**S**	122	Th
982	23 April 1574	F	112	F
983	12 April 1575	Tu	101	S
984*	† 31 March 1576	S	90	**S**
985	21 March 1577	Th	79	Tu
986*	10 March 1578	M	68	W
987	28 February 1579	S	58	Th
988	† 17 February 1580	W	47	F
989*	5 February 1581	**S**	35	**S**
990	26 January 1582	F	25	M

*A Kabisa Year   † A Leap Year

Hijra Year	Christian date of 1 Muharram	Day on which 1 Muharram fell	Number of days elapsed in the Christian Year	Day on which the Christian Year began (O.S. in brackets)	
991	25 January 1583	Tu	24	S	(Tu)
992*	† 14 January 1584	S	13	**S**	(W)
993	3 January 1585	Th	2	Tu	(F)
994	23 December 1585	M	356	Tu	(F)
995*	12 December 1586	F	345	W	(S)
996	2 December 1587	W	335	Th	(**S**)
997*	† 20 November 1588	**S**	324	F	(M)
998	10 November 1589	F	313	**S**	(W)
999	30 October 1590	Tu	302	M	(Th)
1000*	19 October 1591	S	291	Tu	(F)
1001	† 8 October 1592	Th	281	W	(S)
1002	27 September 1593	M	269	F	(M)
1003*	16 September 1594	F	258	S	(Tu)
1004	6 September 1595	W	248	**S**	(W)
1005 ·	† 25 August 1596	**S**	237	M	(Th)
1006*	14 August 1597	Th	225	W	(S)
1007	4 August 1598	Tu	215	Th	(**S**)
1008*	24 July 1599	S	204	F	(M)
1009	† 13 July 1600	Th	194	S	(Tu)
1010	2 July 1601	M	182	M	(Th)
1011*	21 June 1602	F	171	Tu	(F)
1012	11 June 1603	W	161	W	(S)
1013	† 30 May 1604	**S**	150	Th	(**S**)
1014*	19 May 1605	Th	138	S	(Tu)
1015	9 May 1606	Tu	128	**S**	(W)
1016*	28 April 1607	S	117	M	(Th)
1017	† 17 April 1608	Th	107	Tu	(F)
1018	6 April 1609	M	95	Th	(**S**)
1019*	26 March 1610	F	84	F	(M)
1020	16 March 1611	W	74	S	(Tu)

*A *Kabisa Year*   † A *Leap Year*

Hijra Year	Christian date of 1 Muharram	Day on which 1 Muharram fell	Number of days elapsed in the Christian Year	Day on which the Christian Year began (O.S. in brackets)	
1021	† 4 March 1612	S	63	S	(W)
1022*	21 February 1613	Th	51	Tu	(F)
1023	11 February 1614	Tu	41	W	(S)
1024	31 January 1615	S	30	Th	(S)
1025*	† 20 January 1616	W	19	F	(M)
1026	9 January 1617	M	8	S	(W)
1027*	29 December 1617	F	362	S	(W)
1028	19 December 1618	W	352	M	(Th)
1029	8 December 1619	S	341	Tu	(F)
1030*	† 26 November 1620	Th	330	W	(S)
1031	16 November 1621	Tu	319	F	(M)
1032	5 November 1622	S	308	S	(Tu)
1033*	25 October 1623	W	297	S	(W)
1034	† 14 October 1624	M	287	M	(Th)
1035	3 October 1625	F	275	W	(S)
1036*	22 September 1626	Tu	264	Th	(S)
1037	12 September 1627	S	254	F	(M)
1038*	† 31 August 1628	Th	243	S	(Tu)
1039	21 August 1629	Tu	232	M	(Th)
1040	10 August 1630	S	221	Tu	(F)
1041*	30 July 1631	W	210	W	(S)
1042	† 19 July 1632	M	200	Th	(S)
1043	8 July 1633	F	188	S	(Tu)
1044*	27 June 1634	Tu	177	S	(W)
1045	17 June 1635	S	167	M	(Th)
1046*	† 5 June 1636	Th	156	Tu	(F)
1047	26 May 1637	Tu	145	Th	(S)
1048	15 May 1638	S	134	F	(M)
1049*	4 May 1639	W	123	S	(Tu)
1050	† 23 April 1640	M	113	S	(W)

*A Kabisa Year † A Leap Year

Hijra Year	Christian date of 1 Muharram	Day on which 1 Muharram fell	Number of days elapsed in the Christian Year	Day on which the Christian Year began (O.S. in brackets)	
1051	12 April 1641	F	101	Tu	(F)
1052*	1 April 1642	Tu	90	W	(S)
1053	22 March 1643	S	80	Th	(S)
1054	† 10 March 1644	Th	69	F	(M)
1055*	27 February 1645	M	57	S	(W)
1056	17 February 1646	S	47	M	(Th)
1057*	6 February 1647	W	36	Tu	(F)
1058	† 27 January 1648	M	26	W	(S)
1059	15 January 1649	F	14	F	(M)
1060*	4 January 1650	Tu	3	S	(Tu)
1061	25 December 1650	S	358	S	(Tu)
1062	14 December 1651	Th	347	S	(W)
1063*	† 2 December 1652	M	336	M	(Th)
1064	22 November 1653	S	325	W	(S)
1065	11 November 1654	W	314	Th	(S)
1066*	31 October 1655	S	303	F	(M)
1067	† 20 October 1656	F	293	S	(Tu)
1068*	9 October 1657	Tu	281	M	(Th)
1069	29 September 1658	S	271	Tu	(F)
1070	18 September 1659	Th	260	W	(S)
1071*	† 6 September 1660	M	249	Th	(S)
1072	27 August 1661	S	238	S	(Tu)
1073	16 August 1662	W	227	S	(W)
1074*	5 August 1663	S	216	M	(Th)
1075	† 25 July 1664	F	206	Tu	(F)
1076*	14 July 1665	Tu	194	Th	(S)
1077	4 July 1666	S	184	F	(M)
1078	23 June 1667	Th	173	S	(Tu)
1079*	† 11 June 1668	M	162	S	(W)
1080	1 June 1669	S	151	Tu	(F)

*A Kabisa Year   † A Leap Year

Hijra Year	Christian date of 1 Muharram	Day on which 1 Muharram fell	Number of days elapsed in the Christian Year	Day on which the Christian Year began (O.S. in brackets)	
1081	21 May 1670	W	140	W	(S)
1082*	10 May 1671	**S**	129	Th	**(S)**
1083	† 29 April 1672	F	119	F	(M)
1084	18 April 1673	Tu	107	**S**	(W)
1085*	7 April 1674	S	96	M	(Th)
1086	28 March 1675	Th	86	Tu	(F)
1087*	† 16 March 1676	M	75	W	(S)
1088	6 March 1677	S	64	F	(M)
1089	23 February 1678	W	53	S	(Tu)
1090*	12 February 1679	**S**	42	**S**	(W)
1091	† 2 February 1680	F	32	M	(Th)
1092	21 January 1681	Tu	20	W	(S)
1093*	10 January 1682	S	9	Th	**(S)**
1094	31 December 1682	Th	364	Th	**(S)**
1095	20 December 1683	M	353	F	(M)
1096*	† 8 December 1684	F	342	S	(Tu)
1097	28 November 1685	W	331	M	(Th)
1098*	17 November 1686	**S**	320	Tu	(F)
1099	7 November 1687	F	310	W	(S)
1100	† 26 October 1688	Tu	299	Th	**(S)**
1101*	15 October 1689	S	287	S	(Tu)
1102	5 October 1690	Th	277	**S**	(W)
1103	24 September 1691	M	266	M	(Th)
1104*	† 12 September 1692	F	255	Tu	(F)
1105	2 September 1693	W	244	Th	**(S)**
1106*	22 August 1694	**S**	233	F	(M)
1107	12 August 1695	F	223	S	(Tu)
1108	† 31 July 1696	Tu	212	**S**	(W)
1109*	20 July 1697	S	200	Tu	(F)
1110	10 July 1698	Th	190	W	(S)

*A Kabisa Year   † A Leap Year

Hijra Year	Christian date of 1 Muharram	Day on which 1 Muharram fell	Number of days elapsed in the Christian Year	Day on which the Christian Year began (O.S. in brackets)	
1111	29 June 1699	M	179	Th	(**S**)
1112*	18 June 1700	F	168	F	(M)
1113	8 June 1701	W	158	S	(W)
1114	28 May 1702	**S**	147	**S**	(Th)
1115*	17 May 1703	Th	136	M	(F)
1116	† 6 May 1704	Tu	126	Tu	(S)
1117*	25 April 1705	S	114	Th	(M)
1118	15 April 1706	Th	104	F	(Tu)
1119	4 April 1707	M	93	S	(W)
1120*	† 23 March 1708	F	82	**S**	(Th)
1121	13 March 1709	W	71	Tu	(S)
1122	2 March 1710	**S**	60	W	(**S**)
1123*	19 February 1711	Th	49	Th	(M)
1124	† 9 February 1712	Tu	39	F	(Tu)
1125	28 January 1713	S	27	**S**	(Th)
1126*	17 January 1714	W	16	M	(F)
1127	7 January 1715	M	6	Tu	(S)
1128*	27 December 1715	F	360	Tu	(S)
1129	† 16 December 1716	W	350	W	(**S**)
1130	5 December 1717	**S**	338	F	(Tu)
1131*	24 November 1718	Th	327	S	(W)
1132	14 November 1719	Tu	317	**S**	(Th)
1133	† 2 November 1720	S	306	M	(F)
1134*	22 October 1721	W	294	W	(**S**)
1135	12 October 1722	M	284	Th	(M)
1136*	1 October 1723	F	273	F	(Tu)
1137	† 20 September 1724	W	263	S	(W)
1138	9 September 1725	**S**	251	M	(F)
1139*	29 August 1726	Th	240	Tu	(S)
1140	19 August 1727	Tu	230	W	(**S**)

*A Kabisa Year   † A Leap Year

Hijra Year	Christian date of 1 Muharram	Day on which 1 Muharram fell	Number of days elapsed in the Christian Year	Day on which the Christian Year began (O.S. in brackets)	
1141	† 7 August 1728	S	219	Th	(M)
1142*	27 July 1729	W	207	S	(W)
1143	17 July 1730	M	197	**S**	(Th)
1144	6 July 1731	F	186	M	(F)
1145*	† 24 June 1732	Tu	175	Tu	(S)
1146	14 June 1733	**S**	164	Th	(M)
1147*	3 June 1734	Th	153	F	(Tu)
1148	24 May 1735	Tu	143	S	(W)
1149	† 12 May 1736	S	132	**S**	(Th)
1150*	1 May 1737	W	120	Tu	(S)
1151	21 April 1738	M	110	W	**(S)**
1152	10 April 1739	F	99	Th	(M)
1153*	† 29 March 1740	Tu	88	F	(Tu)
1154	19 March 1741	**S**	77	**S**	(Th)
1155	8 March 1742	Th	66	M	(F)
1156*	25 February 1743	M	55	Tu	(S)
1157	† 15 February 1744	S	45	W	**(S)**
1158*	3 February 1745	W	33	F	(Tu)
1159	24 January 1746	M	23	S	(W)
1160	13 January 1747	F	12	**S**	(Th)
1161*	† 2 January 1748	Tu	1	M	(F)
1162	† 22 December 1748	**S**	356	M	(F)
1163	11 December 1749	Th	344	W	**(S)**
1164*	30 November 1750	M	333	Th	(M)
1165	20 November 1751	S	323	F	(Tu)
1166*	† 8 November 1752	W	312	S	(W)
1167	29 October 1753	M	301	M	
1168	18 October 1754	F	290	Tu	
1169*	7 October 1755	Tu	279	W	
1170	† 26 September 1756	**S**	269	Th	

*A Kabisa Year   † A Leap Year

Hijra Year	Christian date of 1 Muharram	Day on which 1 Muharram fell	Number of days elapsed in the Christian Year	Day on which the Christian Year began
1171	15 September 1757	Th	257	S
1172*	4 September 1758	M	246	S
1173	25 August 1759	S	236	M
1174	† 13 August 1760	W	225	Tu
1175*	2 August 1761	S	213	Th
1176	23 July 1762	F	203	F
1177*	12 July 1763	Tu	192	S
1178	† 1 July 1764	S	182	S
1179	20 June 1765	Th	170	Tu
1180*	9 June 1766	M	159	W
1181	30 May 1767	S	149	Th
1182	† 18 May 1768	W	138	F
1183*	7 May 1769	S	126	S
1184	27 April 1770	F	116	M
1185	16 April 1771	Tu	105	Tu
1186*	† 4 April 1772	S	94	W
1187	25 March 1773	Th	83	F
1188*	14 March 1774	M	72	S
1189	4 March 1775	S	62	S
1190	† 21 February 1776	W	51	M
1191*	9 February 1777	S	39	W
1192	30 January 1778	F	29	Th
1193	19 January 1779	Tu	18	F
1194*	† 8 January 1780	S	7	S
1195	† 28 December 1780	Th	362	S
1196*	17 December 1781	M	350	M
1197	7 December 1782	S	340	Tu
1198	26 November 1783	W	329	W
1199*	† 14 November 1784	S	318	Th
1200	4 November 1785	F	307	S

*A Kabisa Year   † A Leap Year

Hijra Year	Christian date of 1 Muharram	Day on which 1 Muharram fell	Number of days elapsed in the Christian Year	Day on which the Christian Year began
1201	24 October 1786	Tu	296	**S**
1202*	13 October 1787	S	285	M
1203	† 2 October 1788	Th	275	Tu
1204	21 September 1789	M	263	Th
1205*	10 September 1790	F	252	F
1206	31 August 1791	W	242	S
1207*	† 19 August 1792	**S**	231	**S**
1208	9 August 1793	F	220	Tu
1209	29 July 1794	Tu	209	W
1210*	18 July 1795	S	198	Th
1211	† 7 July 1796	Th	188	F
1212	26 June 1797	M	176	**S**
1213*	15 June 1798	F	165	M
1214	5 June 1799	W	155	Tu
1215	25 May 1800	**S**	144	W
1216*	14 May 1801	Th	133	Th
1217	4 May 1802	Tu	123	F
1218*	23 April 1803	S	112	S
1219	† 12 April 1804	Th	102	**S**
1220	1 April 1805	M	90	Tu
1221*	21 March 1806	F	79	W
1222	11 March 1807	W	69	Th
1223	† 28 February 1808	**S**	58	F
1224*	16 February 1809	Th	46	**S**
1225	6 February 1810	Tu	36	M
1226*	26 January 1811	S	25	Tu
1227	† 16 January 1812	Th	15	W
1228	4 January 1813	M	3	F
1229*	24 December 1813	F	357	F
1230	14 December 1814	W	347	S

*A Kabisa Year   † A Leap Year

Hijra Year	Christian date of 1 Muharram	Day on which 1 Muharram fell	Number of days elapsed in the Christian Year	Day on which the Christian Year began
1231	3 December 1815	**S**	336	**S**
1232*	† 21 November 1816	Th	325	M
1233	11 November 1817	Tu	314	W
1234	31 October 1818	S	303	Th
1235*	20 October 1819	W	292	F
1236	† 9 October 1820	M	282	S
1237*	28 September 1821	F	270	M
1238	18 September 1822	W	260	Tu
1239	7 September 1823	**S**	249	W
1240*	† 26 August 1824	Th	238	Th
1241	16 August 1825	Tu	227	S
1242	5 August 1826	S	216	**S**
1243*	25 July 1827	W	205	M
1244	† 14 July 1828	M	195	Tu
1245	3 July 1829	F	183	Th
1246*	22 June 1830	Tu	172	F
1247	12 June 1831	**S**	162	S
1248*	† 31 May 1832	Th	151	**S**
1249	21 May 1833	Tu	140	Tu
1250	10 May 1834	S	129	W
1251*	29 April 1835	W	118	Th
1252	† 18 April 1836	M	108	F
1253	7 April 1837	F	96	**S**
1254*	27 March 1838	Tu	85	M
1255	17 March 1839	**S**	75	Tu
1256*	† 5 March 1840	Th	64	W
1257	23 February 1841	Tu	53	F
1258	12 February 1842	S	42	S
1259*	1 February 1843	W	31	**S**
1260	† 22 January 1844	M	21	M

*A *Kabisa* Year   † A *Leap* Year

Hijra Year	Christian date of 1 Muharram	Day on which 1 Muharram fell	Number of days elapsed in the Christian Year	Day on which the Christian Year began
1261	10 January 1845	F	9	W
1262*	30 December 1845	Tu	363	W
1263	20 December 1846	S	353	Th
1264	9 December 1847	Th	342	F
1265*	† 27 November 1848	M	331	S
1266	17 November 1849	S	320	M
1267*	6 November 1850	W	309	Tu
1268	27 October 1851	M	299	W
1269	† 15 October 1852	F	288	Th
1270*	4 October 1853	Tu	276	S
1271	24 September 1854	S	266	S
1272	13 September 1855	Th	255	M
1273*	† 1 September 1856	M	244	Tu
1274	22 August 1857	S	233	Th
1275	11 August 1858	W	222	F
1276*	31 July 1859	S	211	S
1277	† 20 July 1860	F	201	S
1278*	9 July 1861	Tu	189	Tu
1279	29 June 1862	S	179	W
1280	18 June 1863	Th	168	Th
1281*	† 6 June 1864	M	157	F
1282	27 May 1865	S	146	S
1283	16 May 1866	W	135	M
1284*	5 May 1867	S	124	Tu
1285	† 24 April 1868	F	114	W
1286*	13 April 1869	Tu	102	F
1287	3 April 1870	S	92	S
1288	23 March 1871	Th	81	S
1289*	† 11 March 1872	M	70	M
1290	1 March 1873	S	59	W

*A *Kabisa* Year   † A *Leap* Year

Hijra Year	Christian date of 1 Muharram	Day on which 1 Muharram fell	Number of days elapsed in the Christian Year	Day on which the Christian Year began
1291	18 February 1874	W	48	Th
1292*	7 February 1875	**S**	37	F
1293	† 28 January 1876	F	27	S
1294	16 January 1877	Tu	15	M
1295*	5 January 1878	S	4	Tu
1296	26 December 1878	Th	359	Tu
1297*	15 December 1879	M	348	W
1298	† 4 December 1880	S	338	Th
1299	23 November 1881	W	326	S
1300*	12 November 1882	**S**	315	**S**
1301	2 November 1883	F	305	M
1302	† 21 October 1884	Tu	294	Tu
1303*	10 October 1885	S	282	Th
1304	30 September 1886	Th	272	F
1305	19 September 1887	M	261	S
1306*	† 7 September 1888	F	250	**S**
1307	28 August 1889	W	239	Tu
1308*	17 August 1890	**S**	228	W
1309	7 August 1891	F	218	Th
1310	† 26 July 1892	Tu	207	F
1311*	15 July 1893	S	195	**S**
1312	5 July 1894	Th	185	M
1313	24 June 1895	M	174	Tu
1314*	† 12 June 1896	F	163	W
1315	2 June 1897	W	152	F
1316*	22 May 1898	**S**	141	S
1317	12 May 1899	F	131	**S**
1318	1 May 1900	Tu	120	M
1319*	20 April 1901	S	109	Tu
1320	10 April 1902	Th	99	W

*A Kabisa Year   † A Leap Year

Hijra Year	Christian date of 1 Muharram	Day on which 1 Muharram fell	Number of days elapsed in the Christian Year	Day on which the Christian Year began
1321	30 March 1903	M	88	Th
1322*	† 18 March 1904	F	77	F
1323	8 March 1905	W	66	S
1324	25 February 1906	S	55	M
1325*	14 February 1907	Th	44	Tu
1326	† 4 February 1908	Tu	34	W
1327*	23 January 1909	S	22	F
1328	13 January 1910	Th	12	S
1329	2 January 1911	M	1	S
1330*	22 December 1911	F	355	S
1331	† 11 December 1912	W	345	M
1332	30 November 1913	S	333	W
1333*	19 November 1914	Th	322	Th
1334	9 November 1915	Tu	312	F
1335	† 28 October 1916	S	301	S
1336*	17 October 1917	W	289	M
1337	7 October 1918	M	279	Tu
1338*	26 September 1919	F	268	W
1339	† 15 September 1920	W	258	Th
1340	4 September 1921	S	246	S
1341*	24 August 1922	Th	235	S
1342	14 August 1923	Tu	225	M
1343	† 2 August 1924	S	214	Tu
1344*	22 July 1925	W	202	Th
1345	12 July 1926	M	192	F
1346*	1 July 1927	F	181	S
1347	† 20 June 1928	W	171	S
1348	9 June 1929	S	159	Tu
1349*	29 May 1930	Th	148	W
1350	19 May 1931	Tu	138	Th

*A *Kabisa Year*   † *A Leap Year*

TABLE ONE:
THE HIJRA YEAR AND THE CHRISTIAN YEAR

Hijra Year	Christian date of 1 Muharram	Day on which 1 Muharram fell	Number of days elapsed in the Christian Year	Day on which the Christian Year began
1351	† 7 May 1932	S	127	F
1352*	26 April 1933	W	115	**S**
1353	16 April 1934	M	105	M
1354	5 April 1935	F	94	Tu
1355*	† 24 March 1936	Tu	83	W
1356	14 March 1937	**S**	72	F
1357*	3 March 1938	Th	61	S
1358	21 February 1939	Tu	51	**S**
1359	† 10 February 1940	S	40	M
1360*	29 January 1941	W	28	W
1361	19 January 1942	M	18	Th
1362	8 January 1943	F	7	F
1363*	28 December 1943	Tu	361	F
1364	† 17 December 1944	**S**	351	S
1365	6 December 1945	Th	339	M
1366*	25 November 1946	M	328	Tu
1367	15 November 1947	S	318	W
1368*	† 3 November 1948	W	307	Th
1369	24 October 1949	M	296	S
1370	13 October 1950	F	285	**S**
1371*	2 October 1951	Tu	274	M
1372	† 21 September 1952	**S**	264	Tu
1373	10 September 1953	Th	252	Th
1374*	30 August 1954	M	241	F
1375	20 August 1955	S	231	S
1376*	† 8 August 1956	W	220	**S**
1377	29 July 1957	M	209	Tu
1378	18 July 1958	F	198	W
1379*	7 July 1959	Tu	187	Th
1380	† 26 June 1960	**S**	177	F

*A *Kabisa* Year   † A *Leap* Year

Hijra Year	Christian date of 1 Muharram	Day on which 1 Muharram fell	Number of days elapsed in the Christian Year	Day on which the Christian Year began
1381	15 June 1961	Th	165	**S**
1382*	4 June 1962	M	154	M
1383	25 May 1963	S	144	Tu
1384	† 13 May 1964	W	133	W
1385*	2 May 1965	**S**	121	F
1386	22 April 1966	F	111	S
1387*	11 April 1967	Tu	100	**S**
1388	† 31 March 1968	**S**	90	M
1389	20 March 1969	Th	78	W
1390*	9 March 1970	M	67	Th
1391	27 February 1971	S	57	F
1392	† 16 February 1972	W	46	S
1393*	4 February 1973	**S**	34	M
1394	25 January 1974	F	24	Tu
1395	14 January 1975	Tu	13	W
1396*	† 3 January 1976	S	2	Th
1397	† 23 December 1976	Th	357	Th
1398*	12 December 1977	M	345	S
1399	2 December 1978	S	335	**S**
1400	21 November 1979	W	324	M
1401*	† 9 November 1980	**S**	313	Tu
1402	30 October 1981	F	302	Th
1403	19 October 1982	Tu	291	F
1404*	8 October 1983	S	280	S
1405	† 27 September 1984	Th	270	**S**
1406*	16 September 1985	M	258	Tu
1407	6 September 1986	S	248	W
1408	26 August 1987	W	237	Th
1409*	† 14 August 1988	**S**	226	F
1410	4 August 1989	F	215	**S**

*A *Kabisa Year*   † A *Leap Year*

Hijra Year	Christian date of 1 Muharram	Day on which 1 Muharram fell	Number of days elapsed in the Christian Year	Day on which the Christian Year began
1411	24 July 1990	Tu	204	M
1412*	13 July 1991	S	193	Tu
1413	† 2 July 1992	Th	183	W
1414	21 June 1993	M	171	F
1415*	10 June 1994	F	160	S
1416	31 May 1995	W	150	**S**
1417*	† 19 May 1996	**S**	139	M
1418	9 May 1997	F	128	W
1419	28 April 1998	Tu	117	Th
1420*	17 April 1999	S	106	F
1421	† 6 April 2000	Th	96	S
1422	26 March 2001	M	84	M
1423*	15 March 2002	F	73	Tu
1424	5 March 2003	W	63	W
1425	† 22 February 2004	**S**	52	Th
1426*	10 February 2005	Th	40	S
1427	31 January 2006	Tu	30	**S**
1428*	20 January 2007	S	19	M
1429	† 10 January 2008	Th	9	Tu
1430	† 29 December 2008	M	363	Tu
1431*	18 December 2009	F	351	Th
1432	8 December 2010	W	341	F
1433	27 November 2011	**S**	330	S
1434*	† 15 November 2012	Th	319	**S**
1435	5 November 2013	Tu	308	Tu
1436*	25 October 2014	S	297	W
1437	15 October 2015	Th	287	Th
1438	† 3 October 2016	M	276	F
1439*	22 September 2017	F	264	**S**
1440	12 September 2018	W	254	M

*A Kabisa Year   † A Leap Year

Hijra Year	Christian date of 1 Muharram	Day on which 1 Muharram fell	Number of days elapsed in the Christian Year	Day on which the Christian Year began
1441	1 September 2019	**S**	243	Tu
1442*	† 20 August 2020	Th	232	W
1443	10 August 2021	Tu	221	F
1444	30 July 2022	S	210	S
1445*	19 July 2023	W	199	**S**
1446	† 8 July 2024	M	189	M
1447*	27 June 2025	F	177	W
1448	17 June 2026	W	167	Th
1449	6 June 2027	**S**	156	F
1450*	† 25 May 2028	Th	145	S
1451	15 May 2029	Tu	134	M
1452	4 May 2030	S	123	Tu
1453*	23 April 2031	W	112	W
1454	† 12 April 2032	M	102	Th
1455	1 April 2033	F	90	S
1456*	21 March 2034	Tu	79	**S**
1457	11 March 2035	**S**	69	M
1458*	† 28 February 2036	Th	58	Tu
1459	17 February 2037	Tu	47	Th
1460	6 February 2038	S	36	F
1461*	26 January 2039	W	25	S
1462	† 16 January 2040	M	15	**S**
1463	4 January 2041	F	3	Tu
1464*	24 December 2041	Tu	357	Tu
1465	14 December 2042	**S**	347	W
1466*	3 December 2043	Th	336	Th
1467	† 22 November 2044	Tu	326	F
1468	11 November 2045	S	314	**S**
1469*	31 October 2046	W	303	M
1470	21 October 2047	M	293	Tu

*A *Kabisa* Year   † A *Leap* Year

Hijra Year	Christian date of 1 Muharram	Day on which 1 Muharram fell	Number of days elapsed in the Christian Year	Day on which the Christian Year began
1471	† 9 October 2048	F	282	W
1472*	28 September 2049	Tu	270	F
1473	18 September 2050	**S**	260	S
1474	7 September 2051	Th	249	**S**
1475*	† 26 August 2052	M	238	M
1476	16 August 2053	S	227	W
1477*	5 August 2054	W	216	Th
1478	26 July 2055	M	206	F
1479	† 14 July 2056	F	195	S
1480*	3 July 2057	Tu	183	M
1481	23 June 2058	**S**	173	Tu
1482	12 June 2059	Th	162	W
1483*	† 31 May 2060	M	151	Th
1484	21 May 2061	S	140	S
1485	10 May 2062	W	129	**S**
1486*	29 April 2063	**S**	118	M
1487	† 18 April 2064	F	108	Tu
1488*	7 April 2065	Tu	96	Th
1489	28 March 2066	**S**	86	F
1490	17 March 2067	Th	75	S
1491*	† 5 March 2068	M	64	**S**
1492	23 February 2069	S	53	Tu
1493	12 February 2070	W	42	W
1494*	1 February 2071	**S**	31	Th
1495	† 22 January 2072	F	21	F
1496*	10 January 2073	Tu	9	**S**
1497	31 December 2073	**S**	364	**S**
1498	20 December 2074	Th	353	M
1499*	9 December 2075	M	342	Tu
1500	† 28 November 2076	S	332	W

A Kabisa Year   † A Leap Year

Hijra Year	Christian date of 1 Muharram	Day on which 1 Muharram fell	Number of days elapsed in the Christian Year	Day on which the Christian Year began
1501	17 November 2077	W	320	F
1502*	6 November 2078	**S**	309	S
1503	27 October 2079	F	299	**S**
1504	† 15 October 2080	Tu	288	M
1505*	4 October 2081	S	276	W
1506	24 September 2082	Th	266	Th
1507*	13 September 2083	M	255	F
1508	† 2 September 2084	S	245	S
1509	22 August 2085	W	233	M
1510*	11 August 2086	**S**	222	Tu
1511	1 August 2087	F	212	W
1512	† 20 July 2088	Tu	201	Th
1513*	9 July 2089	S	189	S
1514	29 June 2090	Th	179	**S**
1515	18 June 2091	M	168	M
1516*	† 6 June 2092	F	157	Tu
1517	27 May 2093	W	146	Th
1518*	16 May 2094	**S**	135	F
1519	6 May 2095	F	125	S
1520	† 24 April 2096	Tu	114	**S**
1521*	13 April 2097	S	102	Tu
1522	3 April 2098	Th	92	W
1523	23 March 2099	M	81	Th
1524*	12 March 2100	F	70	F
1525	2 March 2101	W	60	S
1526*	19 February 2102	**S**	49	**S**
1527	9 February 2103	F	39	M
1528	† 29 January 2104	Tu	28	Tu
1529*	17 January 2105	S	16	Th
1530	7 January 2106	Th	6	F

*A *Kabisa Year*   † A *Leap Year*

Hijra Year	Christian date of 1 Muharram	Day on which 1 Muharram fell	Number of days elapsed in the Christian Year	Day on which the Christian Year began
1531	27 December 2106	M	360	F
1532*	16 December 2107	F	349	S
1533	† 5 December 2108	W	339	**S**
1534	24 November 2109	**S**	327	Tu
1535*	13 November 2110	Th	316	W
1536	3 November 2111	Tu	306	Th
1537*	† 22 October 2112	S	295	F
1538	12 October 2113	Th	284	**S**
1539	1 October 2114	M	273	M
1540*	20 September 2115	F	262	Tu
1541	† 9 September 2116	W	252	W
1542	29 August 2117	**S**	240	F
1543*	18 August 2118	Th	229	S
1544	8 August 2119	Tu	219	**S**
1545	† 27 July 2120	S	208	M
1546*	16 July 2121	W	196	W
1547	6 July 2122	M	186	Th
1548*	25 June 2123	F	175	F
1549	† 14 June 2124	W	165	S
1550	3 June 2125	**S**	153	M
1551*	23 May 2126	Th	142	Tu
1552	13 May 2127	Tu	132	W
1553	† 1 May 2128	S	121	Th
1554*	20 April 2129	W	109	S
1555	10 April 2130	M	99	**S**
1556*	30 March 2131	F	88	M
1557	† 19 March 2132	W	78	Tu
1558	8 March 2133	**S**	66	Th
1559*	25 February 2134	Th	55	F
1560	15 February 2135	Tu	45	S

*A Kabisa Year   † A Leap Year

Hijra Year	Christian date of 1 Muharram	Day on which 1 Muharram fell	Number of days elapsed in the Christian Year	Day on which the Christian Year began
1561	† 4 February 2136	S	34	**S**
1562*	23 January 2137	W	22	Tu
1563	13 January 2138	M	12	W
1564	2 January 2139	F	1	Th
1565*	22 December 2139	Tu	355	Th
1566	† 11 December 2140	**S**	345	F
1567*	30 November 2141	Th	333	**S**
1568	20 November 2142	Tu	323	M
1569	9 November 2143	S	312	Tu
1570*	† 28 October 2144	W	301	W
1571	18 October 2145	M	290	F
1572	7 October 2146	F	279	S
1573*	26 September 2147	Tu	268	**S**
1574	† 15 September 2148	**S**	258	M
1575	4 September 2149	Th	246	W
1576*	24 August 2150	M	235	Th
1577	14 August 2151	S	225	F
1578*	† 2 August 2152	W	214	S
1579	23 July 2153	M	203	M
1580	12 July 2154	F	192	Tu
1581*	1 July 2155	Tu	181	W
1582	† 20 June 2156	**S**	171	Th
1583	9 June 2157	Th	159	S
1584*	29 May 2158	M	148	**S**
1585	19 May 2159	S	138	M
1586*	† 7 May 2160	W	127	Tu
1587	27 April 2161	M	116	Th
1588	16 April 2162	F	105	F
1589*	5 April 2163	Tu	94	S
1590	† 25 March 2164	**S**	84	**S**

*A Kabisa Year   † A Leap Year

Hijra Year	Christian date of 1 Muharram	Day on which 1 Muharram fell	Number of days elapsed in the Christian Year	Day on which the Christian Year began
1591	14 March 2165	Th	72	Tu
1592*	3 March 2166	M	61	W
1593	21 February 2167	S	51	Th
1594	† 10 February 2168	W	40	F
1595*	29 January 2169	**S**	28	**S**
1596	19 January 2170	F	18	M
1597*	8 January 2171	Tu	7	Tu
1598	29 December 2171	**S**	362	Tu
1599	† 17 December 2172	Th	351	W
1600*	6 December 2173	M	339	F
1601	26 November 2174	S	329	S
1602	15 November 2175	W	318	**S**
1603*	† 3 November 2176	**S**	307	M
1604	24 October 2177	F	296	W
1605	13 October 2178	Tu	285	Th
1606*	2 October 2179	S	274	F
1607	† 21 September 2180	Th	264	S
1608*	10 September 2181	M	252	M
1609	31 August 2182	S	242	Tu
1610	20 August 2183	W	231	W
1611*	† 8 August 2184	**S**	220	Th
1612	29 July 2185	F	209	S
1613	18 July 2186	Tu	198	**S**
1614*	7 July 2187	S	187	M
1615	† 26 June 2188	Th	177	Tu
1616*	15 June 2189	M	165	Th
1617	5 June 2190	S	155	F
1618	25 May 2191	W	144	S
1619*	† 13 May 2192	**S**	133	**S**
1620	3 May 2193	F	122	Tu

*A *Kabisa* Year   † A *Leap* Year

Hijra Year	Christian date of 1 Muharram	Day on which 1 Muharram fell	Number of days elapsed in the Christian Year	Day on which the Christian Year began
1621	22 April 2194	Tu	111	W
1622*	11 April 2195	S	100	Th
1623	† 31 March 2196	Th	90	F
1624	20 March 2197	M	78	S
1625*	9 March 2198	F	67	M
1626	27 February 2199	W	57	Tu
1627*	16 February 2200	S	46	W
1628	6 February 2201	F	36	Th
1629	26 January 2202	Tu	25	F
1630*	15 January 2203	S	14	S
1631	† 5 January 2204	Th	4	S
1632	† 24 December 2204	M	358	S
1633*	13 December 2205	F	346	Tu
1634	3 December 2206	W	336	W
1635	22 November 2207	S	325	Th
1636*	† 10 November 2208	Th	314	F
1637	31 October 2209	Tu	303	S
1638*	20 October 2210	S	292	M
1639	10 October 2211	Th	282	Tu
1640	† 28 September 2212	M	271	W
1641*	17 September 2213	F	259	F
1642	7 September 2214	W	249	S
1643	27 August 2215	S	238	S
1644*	† 15 August 2216	Th	227	M
1645	5 August 2217	Tu	216	W
1646*	25 July 2218	S	205	Th
1647	15 July 2219	Th	195	F
1648	† 3 July 2220	M	184	S
1649*	22 June 2221	F	172	M
1650	12 June 2222	W	162	Tu

*A Kabisa Year   † A Leap Year

THE ISLAMIC MONTHS AND DAYS OF THE YEAR

❖

MUHARRAM Day of the		SAFAR Day of the		RABI' AL-AWWAL Day of the	
Month	Year	Month	Year	Month	Year
1	1	1	31	1	60
2	2	2	32	2	61
3	3	3	33	3	62
4	4	4	34	4	63
5	5	5	35	5	64
6	6	6	36	6	65
7	7	7	37	7	66
8	8	8	38	8	67
9	9	9	39	9	68
10	10	10	40	10	69
11	11	11	41	11	70
12	12	12	42	12	71
13	13	13	43	13	72
14	14	14	44	14	73
15	15	15	45	15	74
16	16	16	46	16	75
17	17	17	47	17	76
18	18	18	48	18	77
19	19	19	49	19	78
20	20	20	50	20	79
21	21	21	51	21	80
22	22	22	52	22	81
23	23	23	53	23	82
24	24	24	54	24	83
25	25	25	55	25	84
26	26	26	56	26	85
27	27	27	57	27	86
28	28	28	58	28	87
29	29	29	59	29	88
30	30	—	—	30	89

RABI' AL-THANI		JUMADA AL-ULA		JUMADA AL-AKHIRA	
Day of the		Day of the		Day of the	
Month	Year	Month	Year	Month	Year
1	90	1	119	1	149
2	91	2	120	2	150
3	92	3	121	3	151
4	93	4	122	4	152
5	94	5	123	5	153
6	95	6	124	6	154
7	96	7	125	7	155
8	97	8	126	8	156
9	98	9	127	9	157
10	99	10	128	10	158
11	100	11	129	11	159
12	101	12	130	12	160
13	102	13	131	13	161
14	103	14	132	14	162
15	104	15	133	15	163
16	105	16	134	16	164
17	106	17	135	17	165
18	107	18	136	18	166
19	108	19	137	19	167
20	109	20	138	20	168
21	110	21	139	21	169
22	111	22	140	22	170
23	112	23	141	23	171
24	113	24	142	24	172
25	114	25	143	25	173
26	115	26	144	26	174
27	116	27	145	27	175
28	117	28	146	28	176
29	118	29	147	29	177
—	—	30	148	—	—

RAJAB Day of the		SHA'BAN Day of the		RAMADHAN Day of the	
Month	Year	Month	Year	Month	Year
1	178	1	208	1	237
2	179	2	209	2	238
3	180	3	210	3	239
4	181	4	211	4	240
5	182	5	212	5	241
6	183	6	213	6	242
7	184	7	214	7	243
8	185	8	215	8	244
9	186	9	216	9	245
10	187	10	217	10	246
11	188	11	218	11	247
12	189	12	219	12	248
13	190	13	220	13	249
14	191	14	221	14	250
15	192	15	222	15	251
16	193	16	223	16	252
17	194	17	224	17	253
18	195	18	225	18	254
19	196	19	226	19	255
20	197	20	227	20	256
21	198	21	228	21	257
22	199	22	229	22	258
23	200	23	230	23	259
24	201	24	231	24	260
25	202	25	232	25	261
26	203	26	233	26	262
27	204	27	234	27	263
28	205	28	235	28	264
29	206	29	236	29	265
30	207	—	—	30	266

SHAWWAL Day of the		DHU AL-QA'DA Day of the		DHU AL-HIJJA Day of the	
Month	Year	Month	Year	Month	Year
1	267	1	296	1	326
2	268	2	297	2	327
3	269	3	298	3	328
4	270	4	299	4	329
5	271	5	300	5	330
6	272	6	301	6	331
7	273	7	302	7	332
8	274	8	303	8	333
9	275	9	304	9	334
10	276	10	305	10	335
11	277	11	306	11	336
12	278	12	307	12	337
13	279	13	308	13	338
14	280	14	309	14	339
15	281	15	310	15	340
16	282	16	311	16	341
17	283	17	312	17	342
18	284	18	313	18	343
19	285	19	314	19	344
20	286	20	315	20	345
21	287	21	316	21	346
22	288	22	317	22	347
23	289	23	318	23	348
24	290	24	319	24	349
25	291	25	320	25	350
26	292	26	321	26	351
27	293	27	322	27	352
28	294	28	323	28	353
29	295	29	324	29	354
—	—	30	325	(30)	(355)*

*In Kabisa Years only

THE CHRISTIAN MONTHS AND DAYS OF THE YEAR

JANUARY			FEBRUARY			MARCH		
Day of the Year	Common Year	Leap Year	Day of the Year	Common Year	Leap Year	Day of the Year	Common Year	Leap Year
1	1	1	32	1	1	60	1	—
2	2	2	33	2	2	61	2	1
3	3	3	34	3	3	62	3	2
4	4	4	35	4	4	63	4	3
5	5	5	36	5	5	64	5	4
6	6	6	37	6	6	65	6	5
7	7	7	38	7	7	66	7	6
8	8	8	39	8	8	67	8	7
9	9	9	40	9	9	68	9	8
10	10	10	41	10	10	69	10	9
11	11	11	42	11	11	70	11	10
12	12	12	43	12	12	71	12	11
13	13	13	44	13	13	72	13	12
14	14	14	45	14	14	73	14	13
15	15	15	46	15	15	74	15	14
16	16	16	47	16	16	75	16	15
17	17	17	48	17	17	76	17	16
18	18	18	49	18	18	77	18	17
19	19	19	50	19	19	78	19	18
20	20	20	51	20	20	79	20	19
21	21	21	52	21	21	80	21	20
22	22	22	53	22	22	81	22	21
23	23	23	54	23	23	82	23	22
24	24	24	55	24	24	83	24	23
25	25	25	56	25	25	84	25	24
26	26	26	57	26	26	85	26	25
27	27	27	58	27	27	86	27	26
28	28	28	59	28	28	87	28	27
29	29	29	60	—	29	88	29	28
30	30	30				89	30	29
31	31	31				90	31	30
						91	—	31

TABLE THREE:
THE CHRISTIAN MONTHS AND DAYS OF THE YEAR

| | APRIL | | | MAY | | | JUNE | |
Day of the Year	Common Year	Leap Year	Day of the Year	Common Year	Leap Year	Day of the Year	Common Year	Leap Year
91	1	—	121	1	—	152	1	—
92	2	1	122	2	1	153	2	1
93	3	2	123	3	2	154	3	2
94	4	3	124	4	3	155	4	3
95	5	4	125	5	4	156	5	4
96	6	5	126	6	5	157	6	5
97	7	6	127	7	6	158	7	6
98	8	7	128	8	7	159	8	7
99	9	8	129	9	8	160	9	8
100	10	9	130	10	9	161	10	9
101	11	10	131	11	10	162	11	10
102	12	11	132	12	11	163	12	11
103	13	12	133	13	12	164	13	12
104	14	13	134	14	13	165	14	13
105	15	14	135	15	14	166	15	14
106	16	15	136	16	15	167	16	15
107	17	16	137	17	16	168	17	16
108	18	17	138	18	17	169	18	17
109	19	18	139	19	18	170	19	18
110	20	19	140	20	19	171	20	19
111	21	20	141	21	20	172	21	20
112	22	21	142	22	21	173	22	21
113	23	22	143	23	22	174	23	22
114	24	23	144	24	23	175	24	23
115	25	24	145	25	24	176	25	24
116	26	25	146	26	25	177	26	25
117	27	26	147	27	26	178	27	26
118	28	27	148	28	27	179	28	27
119	29	28	149	29	28	180	29	28
120	30	29	150	30	29	181	30	29
121	—	30	151	31	30	182	—	30
			152	—	31			

JULY			AUGUST			SEPTEMBER		
Day of the Year	Common Year	Leap Year	Day of the Year	Common Year	Leap Year	Day of the Year	Common Year	Leap Year
182	1	—	213	1	—	244	1	—
183	2	1	214	2	1	245	2	1
184	3	2	215	3	2	246	3	2
185	4	3	216	4	3	247	4	3
186	5	4	217	5	4	248	5	4
187	6	5	218	6	5	249	6	5
188	7	6	219	7	6	250	7	6
189	8	7	220	8	7	251	8	7
190	9	8	221	9	8	252	9	8
191	10	9	222	10	9	253	10	9
192	11	10	223	11	10	254	11	10
193	12	11	224	12	11	255	12	11
194	13	12	225	13	12	256	13	12
195	14	13	226	14	13	257	14	13
196	15	14	227	15	14	258	15	14
197	16	15	228	16	15	259	16	15
198	17	16	229	17	16	260	17	16
199	18	17	230	18	17	261	18	17
200	19	18	231	19	18	262	19	18
201	20	19	232	20	19	263	20	19
202	21	20	233	21	20	264	21	20
203	22	21	234	22	21	265	22	21
204	23	22	235	23	22	266	23	22
205	24	23	236	24	23	267	24	23
206	25	24	237	25	24	268	25	24
207	26	25	238	26	25	269	26	25
208	27	26	239	27	26	270	27	26
209	28	27	240	28	27	271	28	27
210	29	28	241	29	28	272	29	28
211	30	29	242	30	29	273	30	29
212	31	30	243	31	30	274	—	30
213	—	31	244	—	31			

OCTOBER			NOVEMBER			DECEMBER		
Day of the Year	Common Year	Leap Year	Day of the Year	Common Year	Leap Year	Day of the Year	Common Year	Leap Year
274	1	—	305	1	—	335	1	—
275	2	1	306	2	1	336	2	1
276	3	2	307	3	2	337	3	2
277	4	3	308	4	3	338	4	3
278	5	4	309	5	4	339	5	4
279	6	5	310	6	5	340	6	5
280	7	6	311	7	6	341	7	6
281	8	7	312	8	7	342	8	7
282	9	8	313	9	8	343	9	8
283	10	9	314	10	9	344	10	9
284	11	10	315	11	10	345	11	10
285	12	11	316	12	11	346	12	11
286	13	12	317	13	12	347	13	12
287	14	13	318	14	13	348	14	13
288	15	14	319	15	14	349	15	14
289	16	15	320	16	15	350	16	15
290	17	16	321	17	16	351	17	16
291	18	17	322	18	17	352	18	17
292	19	18	323	19	18	353	19	18
293	20	19	324	20	19	354	20	19
294	21	20	325	21	20	355	21	20
295	22	21	326	22	21	356	22	21
296	23	22	327	23	22	357	23	22
297	24	23	328	24	23	358	24	23
298	25	24	329	25	24	359	25	24
299	26	25	330	26	25	360	26	25
300	27	26	331	27	26	361	27	26
301	28	27	332	28	27	362	28	27
302	29	28	333	29	28	363	29	28
303	30	29	334	30	29	364	30	29
304	31	30	335	—	30	365	31	30
305	—	31				366	—	31

PERPETUAL CALENDAR OF THE DAYS OF THE WEEK IN THE CHRISTIAN YEAR

1. Common Years in which 1 January falls on a Sunday

	January					February					March				
S	1	8	15	22	29	—	5	12	19	26	—	5	12	19	26
M	2	9	16	23	30	—	6	13	20	27	—	6	13	20	27
Tu	3	10	17	24	31	—	7	14	21	28	—	7	14	21	28
W	4	11	18	25	—	1	8	15	22	—	1	8	15	22	29
Th	5	12	19	26	—	2	9	16	23	—	2	9	16	23	30
F	6	13	20	27	—	3	10	17	24	—	3	10	17	24	31
S	7	14	21	28	—	4	11	18	25	—	4	11	18	25	—

	April					May					June				
S	—	2	9	16	23	30	—	7	14	21	28	—	4	11	18	25
M	—	3	10	17	24	—	1	8	15	22	29	—	5	12	19	26
Tu	—	4	11	18	25	—	2	9	16	23	30	—	6	13	20	27
W	—	5	12	19	26	—	3	10	17	24	31	—	7	14	21	28
Th	—	6	13	20	27	—	4	11	18	25	—	1	8	15	22	29
F	—	7	14	21	28	—	5	12	19	26	—	2	9	16	23	30
S	1	8	15	22	29	—	6	13	20	27	—	3	10	17	24	—

	July					August					September				
S	—	2	9	16	23	30	—	6	13	20	27	—	3	10	17	24
M	—	3	10	17	24	31	—	7	14	21	28	—	4	11	18	25
Tu	—	4	11	18	25	—	1	8	15	22	29	—	5	12	19	26
W	—	5	12	19	26	—	2	9	16	23	30	—	6	13	20	27
Th	—	6	13	20	27	—	3	10	17	24	31	—	7	14	21	28
F	—	7	14	21	28	—	4	11	18	25	—	1	8	15	22	29
S	1	8	15	22	29	—	5	12	19	26	—	2	9	16	23	30

	October					November					December				
S	1	8	15	22	29	—	5	12	19	26	—	3	10	17	24	31
M	2	9	16	23	30	—	6	13	20	27	—	4	11	18	25	—
Tu	3	10	17	24	31	—	7	14	21	28	—	5	12	19	26	—
W	4	11	18	25	—	1	8	15	22	29	—	6	13	20	27	—
Th	5	12	19	26	—	2	9	16	23	30	—	7	14	21	28	—
F	6	13	20	27	—	3	10	17	24	—	1	8	15	22	29	—
S	7	14	21	28	—	4	11	18	25	—	2	9	16	23	30	—

2. Leap Years in which 1 January falls on a Sunday

	January					February					March				
S	1	8	15	22	29	—	5	12	19	26	—	4	11	18	25
M	2	9	16	23	30	—	6	13	20	27	—	5	12	19	26
Tu	3	10	17	24	31	—	7	14	21	28	—	6	13	20	27
W	4	11	18	25	—	1	8	15	22	29	—	7	14	21	28
Th	5	12	19	26	—	2	9	16	23	—	1	8	15	22	29
F	6	13	20	27	—	3	10	17	24	—	2	9	16	23	30
S	7	14	21	28	—	4	11	18	25	—	3	10	17	24	31

	April					May					June				
S	1	8	15	22	29	—	6	13	20	27	—	3	10	17	24
M	2	9	16	23	30	—	7	14	21	28	—	4	11	18	25
Tu	3	10	17	24	—	1	8	15	22	29	—	5	12	19	26
W	4	11	18	25	—	2	9	16	23	30	—	6	13	20	27
Th	5	12	19	26	—	3	10	17	24	31	—	7	14	21	28
F	6	13	20	27	—	4	11	18	25	—	1	8	15	22	29
S	7	14	21	28	—	5	12	19	26	—	2	9	16	23	30

	July					August					September				
S	1	8	15	22	29	—	5	12	19	26	—	2	9	16	23	30
M	2	9	16	23	30	—	6	13	20	27	—	3	10	17	24	—
Tu	3	10	17	24	31	—	7	14	21	28	—	4	11	18	25	—
W	4	11	18	25	—	1	8	15	22	29	—	5	12	19	26	—
Th	5	12	19	26	—	2	9	16	23	30	—	6	13	20	27	—
F	6	13	20	27	—	3	10	17	24	31	—	7	14	21	28	—
S	7	14	21	28	—	4	11	18	25	—	1	8	15	22	29	—

	October					November					December				
S	—	7	14	21	28	—	4	11	18	25	—	2	9	16	23	30
M	1	8	15	22	29	—	5	12	19	26	—	3	10	17	24	31
Tu	2	9	16	23	30	—	6	13	20	27	—	4	11	18	25	—
W	3	10	17	24	31	—	7	14	21	28	—	5	12	19	26	—
Th	4	11	18	25	—	1	8	15	22	29	—	6	13	20	27	—
F	5	12	19	26	—	2	9	16	23	30	—	7	14	21	28	—
S	6	13	20	27	—	3	10	17	24	—	1	8	15	22	29	—

3. Common Years in which 1 January falls on a Monday

	January						February						March				
S	—	7	14	21	28		—	4	11	18	25		—	4	11	18	25
M	1	8	15	22	29		—	5	12	19	26		—	5	12	19	26
Tu	2	9	16	23	30		—	6	13	20	27		—	6	13	20	27
W	3	10	17	24	31		—	7	14	21	28		—	7	14	21	28
Th	4	11	18	25	—		1	8	15	22	—		1	8	15	22	29
F	5	12	19	26	—		2	9	16	23	—		2	9	16	23	30
S	6	13	20	27	—		3	10	17	24	—		3	10	17	24	31

	April						May						June				
S	1	8	15	22	29		—	6	13	20	27		—	3	10	17	24
M	2	9	16	23	30		—	7	14	21	28		—	4	11	18	25
Tu	3	10	17	24	—		1	8	15	22	29		—	5	12	19	26
W	4	11	18	25	—		2	9	16	23	30		—	6	13	20	27
Th	5	12	19	26	—		3	10	17	24	31		—	7	14	21	28
F	6	13	20	27	—		4	11	18	25	—		1	8	15	22	29
S	7	14	21	28	—		5	12	19	26	—		2	9	16	23	30

	July						August						September				
S	1	8	15	22	29		—	5	12	19	26		—	2	9	16	23	30
M	2	9	16	23	30		—	6	13	20	27		—	3	10	17	24	—
Tu	3	10	17	24	31		—	7	14	21	28		—	4	11	18	25	—
W	4	11	18	25	—		1	8	15	22	29		—	5	12	19	26	—
Th	5	12	19	26	—		2	9	16	23	30		—	6	13	20	27	—
F	6	13	20	27	—		3	10	17	24	31		—	7	14	21	28	—
S	7	14	21	28	—		4	11	18	25	—		1	8	15	22	29	—

	October						November						December				
S	—	7	14	21	28		—	4	11	18	25		—	2	9	16	23	30
M	1	8	15	22	29		—	5	12	19	26		—	3	10	17	24	31
Tu	2	9	16	23	30		—	6	13	20	27		—	4	11	18	25	—
W	3	10	17	24	31		—	7	14	21	28		—	5	12	19	26	—
Th	4	11	18	25	—		1	8	15	22	29		—	6	13	20	27	—
F	5	12	19	26	—		2	9	16	23	30		—	7	14	21	28	—
S	6	13	20	27	—		3	10	17	24	—		1	8	15	22	29	—

4. Leap Years in which 1 January falls on a Monday

	January					February					March				
S	—	7	14	21	28	—	4	11	18	25	—	3	10	17	24	31
M	1	8	15	22	29	—	5	12	19	26	—	4	11	18	25	—
Tu	2	9	16	23	30	—	6	13	20	27	—	5	12	19	26	—
W	3	10	17	24	31	—	7	14	21	28	—	6	13	20	27	—
Th	4	11	18	25	—	1	8	15	22	29	—	7	14	21	28	—
F	5	12	19	26	—	2	9	16	23	—	1	8	15	22	29	—
S	6	13	20	27	—	3	10	17	24	—	2	9	16	23	30	—

	April					May					June				
S	—	7	14	21	28	—	5	12	19	26	—	2	9	16	23	30
M	1	8	15	22	29	—	6	13	20	27	—	3	10	17	24	—
Tu	2	9	16	23	30	—	7	14	21	28	—	4	11	18	25	—
W	3	10	17	24	—	1	8	15	22	29	—	5	12	19	26	—
Th	4	11	18	25	—	2	9	16	23	30	—	6	13	20	27	—
F	5	12	19	26	—	3	10	17	24	31	—	7	14	21	28	—
S	6	13	20	27	—	4	11	18	25	—	1	8	15	22	29	—

	July					August					September				
S	—	7	14	21	28	—	4	11	18	25	1	8	15	22	29
M	1	8	15	22	29	—	5	12	19	26	2	9	16	23	30
Tu	2	9	16	23	30	—	6	13	20	27	3	10	17	24	—
W	3	10	17	24	31	—	7	14	21	28	4	11	18	25	—
Th	4	11	18	25	—	1	8	15	22	29	5	12	19	26	—
F	5	12	19	26	—	2	9	16	23	30	6	13	20	27	—
S	6	13	20	27	—	3	10	17	24	31	7	14	21	28	—

	October					November					December				
S	—	6	13	20	27	—	3	10	17	24	1	8	15	22	29
M	—	7	14	21	28	—	4	11	18	25	2	9	16	23	30
Tu	1	8	15	22	29	—	5	12	19	26	3	10	17	24	31
W	2	9	16	23	30	—	6	13	20	27	4	11	18	25	—
Th	3	10	17	24	31	—	7	14	21	28	5	12	19	26	—
F	4	11	18	25	—	1	8	15	22	29	6	13	20	27	—
S	5	12	19	26	—	2	9	16	23	30	7	14	21	28	—

5. Common Years in which 1 January falls on a Tuesday

	January					February					March				
S	—	6	13	20	27	—	3	10	17	24	—	3	10	17	24	31
M	—	7	14	21	28	—	4	11	18	25	—	4	11	18	25	—
Tu	1	8	15	22	29	—	5	12	19	26	—	5	12	19	26	—
W	2	9	16	23	30	—	6	13	20	27	—	6	13	20	27	—
Th	3	10	17	24	31	—	7	14	21	28	—	7	14	21	28	—
F	4	11	18	25	—	1	8	15	22	—	1	8	15	22	29	—
S	5	12	19	26	—	2	9	16	23	—	2	9	16	23	30	—

	April					May					June				
S	—	7	14	21	28	—	5	12	19	26	—	2	9	16	23	30
M	1	8	15	22	29	—	6	13	20	27	—	3	10	17	24	—
Tu	2	9	16	23	30	—	7	14	21	28	—	4	11	18	25	—
W	3	10	17	24	—	1	8	15	22	29	—	5	12	19	26	—
Th	4	11	18	25	—	2	9	16	23	30	—	6	13	20	27	—
F	5	12	19	26	—	3	10	17	24	31	—	7	14	21	28	—
S	6	13	20	27	—	4	11	18	25	—	1	8	15	22	29	—

	July					August					September				
S	—	7	14	21	28	—	4	11	18	25	1	8	15	22	29
M	1	8	15	22	29	—	5	12	19	26	2	9	16	23	30
Tu	2	9	16	23	30	—	6	13	20	27	3	10	17	24	—
W	3	10	17	24	31	—	7	14	21	28	4	11	18	25	—
Th	4	11	18	25	—	1	8	15	22	29	5	12	19	26	—
F	5	12	19	26	—	2	9	16	23	30	6	13	20	27	—
S	6	13	20	27	—	3	10	17	24	31	7	14	21	28	—

	October					November					December				
S	—	6	13	20	27	—	3	10	17	24	1	8	15	22	29
M	—	7	14	21	28	—	4	11	18	25	2	9	16	23	30
Tu	1	8	15	22	29	—	5	12	19	26	3	10	17	24	31
W	2	9	16	23	30	—	6	13	20	27	4	11	18	25	—
Th	3	10	17	24	31	—	7	14	21	28	5	12	19	26	—
F	4	11	18	25	—	1	8	15	22	29	6	13	20	27	—
S	5	12	19	26	—	2	9	16	23	30	7	14	21	28	—

6. Leap Years in which 1 January falls on a Tuesday

	January					February					March				
S	—	6	13	20	27	—	3	10	17	24	—	2	9	16	23	30
M	—	7	14	21	28	—	4	11	18	25	—	3	10	17	24	31
Tu	1	8	15	22	29	—	5	12	19	26	—	4	11	18	25	—
W	2	9	16	23	30	—	6	13	20	27	—	5	12	19	26	—
Th	3	10	17	24	31	—	7	14	21	28	—	6	13	20	27	—
F	4	11	18	25	—	1	8	15	22	29	—	7	14	21	28	—
S	5	12	19	26	—	2	9	16	23	—	1	8	15	22	29	—

	April					May					June				
S	—	6	13	20	27	—	4	11	18	25	1	8	15	22	29
M	—	7	14	21	28	—	5	12	19	26	2	9	16	23	30
Tu	1	8	15	22	29	—	6	13	20	27	3	10	17	24	—
W	2	9	16	23	30	—	7	14	21	28	4	11	18	25	—
Th	3	10	17	24	—	1	8	15	22	29	5	12	19	26	—
F	4	11	18	25	—	2	9	16	23	30	6	13	20	27	—
S	5	12	19	26	—	3	10	17	24	31	7	14	21	28	—

	July					August					September				
S	—	6	13	20	27	—	3	10	17	24	31	—	7	14	21	28
M	—	7	14	21	28	—	4	11	18	25	—	1	8	15	22	29
Tu	1	8	15	22	29	—	5	12	19	26	—	2	9	16	23	30
W	2	9	16	23	30	—	6	13	20	27	—	3	10	17	24	—
Th	3	10	17	24	31	—	7	14	21	28	—	4	11	18	25	—
F	4	11	18	25	—	1	8	15	22	29	—	5	12	19	26	—
S	5	12	19	26	—	2	9	16	23	30	—	6	13	20	27	—

	October					November					December				
S	—	5	12	19	26	—	2	9	16	23	30	—	7	14	21	28
M	—	6	13	20	27	—	3	10	17	24	—	1	8	15	22	29
Tu	—	7	14	21	28	—	4	11	18	25	—	2	9	16	23	30
W	1	8	15	22	29	—	5	12	19	26	—	3	10	17	24	31
Th	2	9	16	23	30	—	6	13	20	27	—	4	11	18	25	—
F	3	10	17	24	31	—	7	14	21	28	—	5	12	19	26	—
S	4	11	18	25	—	1	8	15	22	29	—	6	13	20	27	—

7. Common Years in which 1 January falls on a Wednesday

	January					February					March				
S	—	5	12	19	26	—	2	9	16	23	—	2	9	16	23	30
M	—	6	13	20	27	—	3	10	17	24	—	3	10	17	24	31
Tu	—	7	14	21	28	—	4	11	18	25	—	4	11	18	25	—
W	1	8	15	22	29	—	5	12	19	26	—	5	12	19	26	—
Th	2	9	16	23	30	—	6	13	20	27	—	6	13	20	27	—
F	3	10	17	24	31	—	7	14	21	28	—	7	14	21	28	—
S	4	11	18	25	—	1	8	15	22	—	1	8	15	22	29	—

	April					May					June				
S	—	6	13	20	27	—	4	11	18	25	1	8	15	22	29
M	—	7	14	21	28	—	5	12	19	26	2	9	16	23	30
Tu	1	8	15	22	29	—	6	13	20	27	3	10	17	24	—
W	2	9	16	23	30	—	7	14	21	28	4	11	18	25	—
Th	3	10	17	24	—	1	8	15	22	29	5	12	19	26	—
F	4	11	18	25	—	2	9	16	23	30	6	13	20	27	—
S	5	12	19	26	—	3	10	17	24	31	7	14	21	28	—

	July					August					September				
S	—	6	13	20	27	—	3	10	17	24	31	—	7	14	21	28
M	—	7	14	21	28	—	4	11	18	25	—	1	8	15	22	29
Tu	1	8	15	22	29	—	5	12	19	26	—	2	9	16	23	30
W	2	9	16	23	30	—	6	13	20	27	—	3	10	17	24	—
Th	3	10	17	24	31	—	7	14	21	28	—	4	11	18	25	—
F	4	11	18	25	—	1	8	15	22	29	—	5	12	19	26	—
S	5	12	19	26	—	2	9	16	23	30	—	6	13	20	27	—

	October					November					December				
S	—	5	12	19	26	—	2	9	16	23	30	—	7	14	21	28
M	—	6	13	20	27	—	3	10	17	24	—	1	8	15	22	29
Tu	—	7	14	21	28	—	4	11	18	25	—	2	9	16	23	30
W	1	8	15	22	29	—	5	12	19	26	—	3	10	17	24	31
Th	2	9	16	23	30	—	6	13	20	27	—	4	11	18	25	—
F	3	10	17	24	31	—	7	14	21	28	—	5	12	19	26	—
S	4	11	18	25	—	1	8	15	22	29	—	6	13	20	27	—

8. Leap Years in which 1 January falls on a Wednesday

	January						*February*						*March*				
S	—	5	12	19	26		—	2	9	16	23		1	8	15	22	29
M	—	6	13	20	27		—	3	10	17	24		2	9	16	23	30
Tu	—	7	14	21	28		—	4	11	18	25		3	10	17	24	31
W	1	8	15	22	29		—	5	12	19	26		4	11	18	25	—
Th	2	9	16	23	30		—	6	13	20	27		5	12	19	26	—
F	3	10	17	24	31		—	7	14	21	28		6	13	20	27	—
S	4	11	18	25	—		1	8	15	22	29		7	14	21	28	—

	April						*May*						*June*				
S	—	5	12	19	26		—	3	10	17	24	31	—	7	14	21	28
M	—	6	13	20	27		—	4	11	18	25	—	1	8	15	22	29
Tu	—	7	14	21	28		—	5	12	19	26	—	2	9	16	23	30
W	1	8	15	22	29		—	6	13	20	27	—	3	10	17	24	—
Th	2	9	16	23	30		—	7	14	21	28	—	4	11	18	25	—
F	3	10	17	24	—		1	8	15	22	29	—	5	12	19	26	—
S	4	11	18	25	—		2	9	16	23	30	—	6	13	20	27	—

	July						*August*						*September*				
S	—	5	12	19	26		—	2	9	16	23	30	—	6	13	20	27
M	—	6	13	20	27		—	3	10	17	24	31	—	7	14	21	28
Tu	—	7	14	21	28		—	4	11	18	25	—	1	8	15	22	29
W	1	8	15	22	29		—	5	12	19	26	—	2	9	16	23	30
Th	2	9	16	23	30		—	6	13	20	27	—	3	10	17	24	—
F	3	10	17	24	31		—	7	14	21	28	—	4	11	18	25	—
S	4	11	18	25	—		1	8	15	22	29	—	5	12	19	26	—

	October						*November*						*December*				
S	—	4	11	18	25		1	8	15	22	29		—	6	13	20	27
M	—	5	12	19	26		2	9	16	23	30		—	7	14	21	28
Tu	—	6	13	20	27		3	10	17	24	—		1	8	15	22	29
W	—	7	14	21	28		4	11	18	25	—		2	9	16	23	30
Th	1	8	15	22	29		5	12	19	26	—		3	10	17	24	31
F	2	9	16	23	30		6	13	20	27	—		4	11	18	25	—
S	3	10	17	24	31		7	14	21	28	—		5	12	19	26	—

9. Common Years in which 1 January falls on a Thursday

	January						February					March				
S	—	4	11	18	25		1	8	15	22		1	8	15	22	29
M	—	5	12	19	26		2	9	16	23		2	9	16	23	30
Tu	—	6	13	20	27		3	10	17	24		3	10	17	24	31
W	—	7	14	21	28		4	11	18	25		4	11	18	25	—
Th	1	8	15	22	29		5	12	19	26		5	12	19	26	—
F	2	9	16	23	30		6	13	20	27		6	13	20	27	—
S	3	10	17	24	31		7	14	21	28		7	14	21	28	—

	April						May						June				
S	—	5	12	19	26	—	3	10	17	24	31	—	7	14	21	28
M	—	6	13	20	27	—	4	11	18	25	—	1	8	15	22	29
Tu	—	7	14	21	28	—	5	12	19	26	—	2	9	16	23	30
W	1	8	15	22	29	—	6	13	20	27	—	3	10	17	24	—
Th	2	9	16	23	30	—	7	14	21	28	—	4	11	18	25	—
F	3	10	17	24	—	1	8	15	22	29	—	5	12	19	26	—
S	4	11	18	25	—	2	9	16	23	30	—	6	13	20	27	—

	July						August						September				
S	—	5	12	19	26	—	2	9	16	23	30	—	6	13	20	27
M	—	6	13	20	27	—	3	10	17	24	31	—	7	14	21	28
Tu	—	7	14	21	28	—	4	11	18	25	—	1	8	15	22	29
W	1	8	15	22	29	—	5	12	19	26	—	2	9	16	23	30
Th	2	9	16	23	30	—	6	13	20	27	—	3	10	17	24	—
F	3	10	17	24	31	—	7	14	21	28	—	4	11	18	25	—
S	4	11	18	25	—	1	8	15	22	29	—	5	12	19	26	—

	October						November						December				
S	—	4	11	18	25		1	8	15	22	29	—	6	13	20	27
M	—	5	12	19	26		2	9	16	23	30	—	7	14	21	28
Tu	—	6	13	20	27		3	10	17	24	—	1	8	15	22	29
W	—	7	14	21	28		4	11	18	25	—	2	9	16	23	30
Th	1	8	15	22	29		5	12	19	26	—	3	10	17	24	31
F	2	9	16	23	30		6	13	20	27	—	4	11	18	25	—
S	3	10	17	24	31		7	14	21	28	—	5	12	19	26	—

10. Leap Years in which 1 January falls on a Thursday

	January						February						March				
S	—	4	11	18	25		1	8	15	22	29		—	7	14	21	28
M	—	5	12	19	26		2	9	16	23	—		1	8	15	22	29
Tu	—	6	13	20	27		3	10	17	24	—		2	9	16	23	30
W	—	7	14	21	28		4	11	18	25	—		3	10	17	24	31
Th	1	8	15	22	29		5	12	19	26	—		4	11	18	25	—
F	2	9	16	23	30		6	13	20	27	—		5	12	19	26	—
S	3	10	17	24	31		7	14	21	28	—		6	13	20	27	—

	April						May						June				
S	—	4	11	18	25	—	2	9	16	23	30		—	6	13	20	27
M	—	5	12	19	26	—	3	10	17	24	31		—	7	14	21	28
Tu	—	6	13	20	27	—	4	11	18	25	—		1	8	15	22	29
W	—	7	14	21	28	—	5	12	19	26	—		2	9	16	23	30
Th	1	8	15	22	29	—	6	13	20	27	—		3	10	17	24	—
F	2	9	16	23	30	—	7	14	21	28	—		4	11	18	25	—
S	3	10	17	24	—	1	8	15	22	29	—		5	12	19	26	—

	July						August						September				
S	—	4	11	18	25		1	8	15	22	29		—	5	12	19	26
M	—	5	12	19	26		2	9	16	23	30		—	6	13	20	27
Tu	—	6	13	20	27		3	10	17	24	31		—	7	14	21	28
W	—	7	14	21	28		4	11	18	25	—		1	8	15	22	29
Th	1	8	15	22	29		5	12	19	26	—		2	9	16	23	30
F	2	9	16	23	30		6	13	20	27	—		3	10	17	24	—
S	3	10	17	24	31		7	14	21	28	—		4	11	18	25	—

	October						November						December				
S	—	3	10	17	24	31	—	7	14	21	28		—	5	12	19	26
M	—	4	11	18	25	—	1	8	15	22	29		—	6	13	20	27
Tu	—	5	12	19	26	—	2	9	16	23	30		—	7	14	21	28
W	—	6	13	20	27	—	3	10	17	24	—		1	8	15	22	29
Th	—	7	14	21	28	—	4	11	18	25	—		2	9	16	23	30
F	1	8	15	22	29	—	5	12	19	26	—		3	10	17	24	31
S	2	9	16	23	30	—	6	13	20	27	—		4	11	18	25	—

11. Common Years in which 1 January falls on a Friday

	January					
S	—	3	10	17	24	31
M	—	4	11	18	25	—
Tu	—	5	12	19	26	—
W	—	6	13	20	27	—
Th	—	7	14	21	28	—
F	1	8	15	22	29	—
S	2	9	16	23	30	—

	February				
—	7	14	21	28
1	8	15	22	—
2	9	16	23	—
3	10	17	24	—
4	11	18	25	—
5	12	19	26	—
6	13	20	27	—

	March				
—	7	14	21	28
1	8	15	22	29
2	9	16	23	30
3	10	17	24	31
4	11	18	25	—
5	12	19	26	—
6	13	20	27	—

	April				
S	—	4	11	18	25
M	—	5	12	19	26
Tu	—	6	13	20	27
W	—	7	14	21	28
Th	1	8	15	22	29
F	2	9	16	23	30
S	3	10	17	24	—

	May					
—	2	9	16	23	30
—	3	10	17	24	31
—	4	11	18	25	—
—	5	12	19	26	—
—	6	13	20	27	—
—	7	14	21	28	—
1	8	15	22	29	—

	June			
—	6	13	20	27
—	7	14	21	28
1	8	15	22	29
2	9	16	23	30
3	10	17	24	—
4	11	18	25	—
5	12	19	26	—

	July			
S	—	4	11	18	25
M	—	5	12	19	26
Tu	—	6	13	20	27
W	—	7	14	21	28
Th	1	8	15	22	29
F	2	9	16	23	30
S	3	10	17	24	31

	August				
1	8	15	22	29
2	9	16	23	30
3	10	17	24	31
4	11	18	25	—
5	12	19	26	—
6	13	20	27	—
7	14	21	28	—

	September			
—	5	12	19	26
—	6	13	20	27
—	7	14	21	28
1	8	15	22	29
2	9	16	23	30
3	10	17	24	—
4	11	18	25	—

	October				
S	—	3	10	17	24	31
M	—	4	11	18	25	—
Tu	—	5	12	19	26	—
W	—	6	13	20	27	—
Th	—	7	14	21	28	—
F	1	8	15	22	29	—
S	2	9	16	23	30	—

	November				
—	7	14	21	28
1	8	15	22	29
2	9	16	23	30
3	10	17	24	—
4	11	18	25	—
5	12	19	26	—
6	13	20	27	—

	December				
—	5	12	19	26
—	6	13	20	27
—	7	14	21	28
1	8	15	22	29
2	9	16	23	30
3	10	17	24	31
4	11	18	25	—

12. Leap Years in which 1 January falls on a Friday

January						
S	—	3	10	17	24	31
M	—	4	11	18	25	—
Tu	—	5	12	19	26	—
W	—	6	13	20	27	—
Th	—	7	14	21	28	—
F	1	8	15	22	29	—
S	2	9	16	23	30	—

February					
—	7	14	21	28	
1	8	15	22	29	
2	9	16	23	—	
3	10	17	24	—	
4	11	18	25	—	
5	12	19	26	—	
6	13	20	27	—	

March					
—	6	13	20	27	
—	7	14	21	28	
1	8	15	22	29	
2	9	16	23	30	
3	10	17	24	31	
4	11	18	25	—	
5	12	19	26	—	

April					
S	—	3	10	17	24
M	—	4	11	18	25
Tu	—	5	12	19	26
W	—	6	13	20	27
Th	—	7	14	21	28
F	1	8	15	22	29
S	2	9	16	23	30

May					
1	8	15	22	29	
2	9	16	23	30	
3	10	17	24	31	
4	11	18	25	—	
5	12	19	26	—	
6	13	20	27	—	
7	14	21	28	—	

June					
—	5	12	19	26	
—	6	13	20	27	
—	7	14	21	28	
1	8	15	22	29	
2	9	16	23	30	
3	10	17	24	—	
4	11	18	25	—	

July						
S	—	3	10	17	24	31
M	—	4	11	18	25	—
Tu	—	5	12	19	26	—
W	—	6	13	20	27	—
Th	—	7	14	21	28	—
F	1	8	15	22	29	—
S	2	9	16	23	30	—

August					
—	7	14	21	28	
1	8	15	22	29	
2	9	16	23	30	
3	10	17	24	31	
4	11	18	25	—	
5	12	19	26	—	
6	13	20	27	—	

September					
—	4	11	18	25	
—	5	12	19	26	
—	6	13	20	27	
—	7	14	21	28	
1	8	15	22	29	
2	9	16	23	30	
3	10	17	24	—	

October					
S	—	2	9	16	23	30
M	—	3	10	17	24	31
Tu	—	4	11	18	25	—
W	—	5	12	19	26	—
Th	—	6	13	20	27	—
F	—	7	14	21	28	—
S	1	8	15	22	29	—

November					
—	6	13	20	27	
—	7	14	21	28	
1	8	15	22	29	
2	9	16	23	30	
3	10	17	24	—	
4	11	18	25	—	
5	12	19	26	—	

December					
—	4	11	18	25	
—	5	12	19	26	
—	6	13	20	27	
—	7	14	21	28	
1	8	15	22	29	
2	9	16	23	30	
3	10	17	24	31	

13. Common Years in which 1 January falls on a Saturday

			January							February							March			
S	—	2	9	16	23	30		—	6	13	20	27			—	6	13	20	27	
M	—	3	10	17	24	31		—	7	14	21	28			—	7	14	21	28	
Tu	—	4	11	18	25	—		1	8	15	22	—			1	8	15	22	29	
W	—	5	12	19	26	—		2	9	16	23	—			2	9	16	23	30	
Th	—	6	13	20	27	—		3	10	17	24	—			3	10	17	24	31	
F	—	7	14	21	28	—		4	11	18	25	—			4	11	18	25	—	
S	1	8	15	22	29	—		5	12	19	26	—			5	12	19	26	—	

			April							May							June			
S		—	3	10	17	24		1	8	15	22	29			—	5	12	19	26	
M		—	4	11	18	25		2	9	16	23	30			—	6	13	20	27	
Tu		—	5	12	19	26		3	10	17	24	31			—	7	14	21	28	
W		—	6	13	20	27		4	11	18	25	—			1	8	15	22	29	
Th		—	7	14	21	28		5	12	19	26	—			2	9	16	23	30	
F		1	8	15	22	29		6	13	20	27	—			3	10	17	24	—	
S		2	9	16	23	30		7	14	21	28	—			4	11	18	25	—	

			July							August							September			
S	—	3	10	17	24	31		—	7	14	21	28			—	4	11	18	25	
M	—	4	11	18	25	—		1	8	15	22	29			—	5	12	19	26	
Tu	—	5	12	19	26	—		2	9	16	23	30			—	6	13	20	27	
W	—	6	13	20	27	—		3	10	17	24	31			—	7	14	21	28	
Th	—	7	14	21	28	—		4	11	18	25	—			1	8	15	22	29	
F	1	8	15	22	29	—		5	12	19	26	—			2	9	16	23	30	
S	2	9	16	23	30	—		6	13	20	27	—			3	10	17	24	—	

			October							November							December			
S	—	2	9	16	23	30		—	6	13	20	27			—	4	11	18	25	
M	—	3	10	17	24	31		—	7	14	21	28			—	5	12	19	26	
Tu	—	4	11	18	25	—		1	8	15	22	29			—	6	13	20	27	
W	—	5	12	19	26	—		2	9	16	23	30			—	7	14	21	28	
Th	—	6	13	20	27	—		3	10	17	24	—			1	8	15	22	29	
F	—	7	14	21	28	—		4	11	18	25	—			2	9	16	23	30	
S	1	8	15	22	29	—		5	12	19	26	—			3	10	17	24	31	

14. Leap Years in which 1 January falls on a Saturday

January

S	—	2	9	16	23	30
M	—	3	10	17	24	31
Tu	—	4	11	18	25	—
W	—	5	12	19	26	—
Th	—	6	13	20	27	—
F	—	7	14	21	28	—
S	1	8	15	22	29	—

February

S	—	6	13	20	27	
M	—	7	14	21	28	
Tu	1	8	15	22	29	
W	2	9	16	23	—	
Th	3	10	17	24	—	
F	4	11	18	25	—	
S	5	12	19	26	—	

March

S	—	5	12	19	26	
M	—	6	13	20	27	
Tu	—	7	14	21	28	
W	1	8	15	22	29	
Th	2	9	16	23	30	
F	3	10	17	24	31	
S	4	11	18	25	—	

April

S	—	2	9	16	23	30
M	—	3	10	17	24	—
Tu	—	4	11	18	25	—
W	—	5	12	19	26	—
Th	—	6	13	20	27	—
F	—	7	14	21	28	—
S	1	8	15	22	29	—

May

S	—	7	14	21	28	
M	1	8	15	22	29	
Tu	2	9	16	23	30	
W	3	10	17	24	31	
Th	4	11	18	25	—	
F	5	12	19	26	—	
S	6	13	20	27	—	

June

S	—	4	11	18	25	
M	—	5	12	19	26	
Tu	—	6	13	20	27	
W	—	7	14	21	28	
Th	1	8	15	22	29	
F	2	9	16	23	30	
S	3	10	17	24	—	

July

S	—	2	9	16	23	30
M	—	3	10	17	24	31
Tu	—	4	11	18	25	—
W	—	5	12	19	26	—
Th	—	6	13	20	27	—
F	—	7	14	21	28	—
S	1	8	15	22	29	—

August

S	—	6	13	20	27	
M	—	7	14	21	28	
Tu	1	8	15	22	29	
W	2	9	16	23	30	
Th	3	10	17	24	31	
F	4	11	18	25	—	
S	5	12	19	26	—	

September

S	—	3	10	17	24	
M	—	4	11	18	25	
Tu	—	5	12	19	26	
W	—	6	13	20	27	
Th	—	7	14	21	28	
F	1	8	15	22	29	
S	2	9	16	23	30	

October

S	1	8	15	22	29	
M	2	9	16	23	30	
Tu	3	10	17	24	31	
W	4	11	18	25	—	
Th	5	12	19	26	—	
F	6	13	20	27	—	
S	7	14	21	28	—	

November

S	—	5	12	19	26	
M	—	6	13	20	27	
Tu	—	7	14	21	28	
W	1	8	15	22	29	
Th	2	9	16	23	30	
F	3	10	17	24	—	
S	4	11	18	25	—	

December

S	—	3	10	17	24	31
M	—	4	11	18	25	—
Tu	—	5	12	19	26	—
W	—	6	13	20	27	—
Th	—	7	14	21	28	—
F	1	8	15	22	29	—
S	2	9	16	23	30	—

CALENDAR FOR OCTOBER TO DECEMBER, AD 1582—NEW STLYE

The first nine months of the Christian Year 1582 follow the table of Common Years in which 1 January falls on a Monday, as shown in TABLE FOUR, 3, with the Days of the Year as shown in TABLE THREE. A special table is required, therefore, only for October, November and December, as follows.

OCTOBER	Day of the		NOVEMBER	Day of the		DECEMBER	Day of the	
Year	Month	Week	Year	Month	Week	Year	Month	Week
274	1	M	295	1	M	325	1	W
275	2	Tu	296	2	Tu	326	2	Th
276	3	W	297	3	W	327	3	F
277	4	Th	298	4	Th	328	4	S
			299	5	F	329	5	**S**
	NEW STYLE		300	6	S	330	6	M
278	15	F	301	7	**S**	331	7	Tu
279	16	S	302	8	M	332	8	W
280	17	**S**	303	9	Tu	333	9	Th
281	18	M	304	10	W	334	10	F
282	19	Tu	305	11	Th	335	11	S
283	20	W	306	12	F	336	12	**S**
284	21	Th	307	13	S	337	13	M
285	22	F	308	14	**S**	338	14	Tu
286	23	S	309	15	M	339	15	W
287	24	**S**	310	16	Tu	340	16	Th
288	25	M	311	17	W	341	17	F
289	26	Tu	312	18	Th	342	18	S
290	27	W	313	19	F	343	19	**S**
291	28	Th	314	20	S	344	20	M
292	29	F	315	21	**S**	345	21	Tu
293	30	S	316	22	M	346	22	W
294	31	**S**	317	23	Tu	347	23	Th
			318	24	W	348	24	F
			319	25	Th	349	25	S
			320	26	F	350	26	**S**
			321	27	S	351	27	M
			322	28	**S**	352	28	Tu
			323	29	M	353	29	W
			324	30	Tu	354	30	Th
						355	31	F

THE PRINCIPAL ISLAMIC FESTIVALS

1 Muharram:	New Year's Day.
10 Muharram:	al-Ashura.
12 Rabi' al-Awal:	Maulid al-Nabi (Birth of the Prophet Muhammad).
27 Rajab:	Isra al-Miraj (Ascent of the Prophet Muhammad into Heaven).
1 Ramadhan:	The beginning of the month of fasting.
27 Ramadhan:	Lailat al-Qadr ('The Night of Power').
1 Shawwal:	'Id al-Fitr. (The celebration of this festival commonly continues for two to three days.)
10 Dhu al-Hijja:	'Id al-Hajj. (This festival commonly continues for at least two days.)

$\mathcal{T}$HE PRINCIPAL FIXED CHRISTIAN FESTIVALS

1 January:	New Year's Day.
6 January:	Epiphany.
25 March:	The Annunciation of the Blessed Virgin Mary.
29 June:	Saints Peter and Paul.
15 August:	The Assumption of the Blessed Virgin Mary.
1 November:	All Saints' Day.
2 November:	All Souls' Day.
25 December:	Christmas Day.

Movable Christian Festivals (Gregorian Calendar)

	Ash Wednesday	Easter	Ascension	Pentecost	Corpus Christi	First Sunday in Advent
1995	1 March	16 April	25 May	4 June	15 June	3 Dec.
1996	21 Feb.	7 April	16 May	26 May	6 June	1 Dec.
1997	12 Feb.	30 March	8 May	18 May	29 May	30 Nov.
1998	25 Feb.	12 April	21 May	31 May	11 June	29 Nov.
1999	17 Feb.	4 April	13 May	23 May	3 June	28 Nov.
2000	9 March	23 April	1 June	11 June	22 June	3 Dec.
2001	28 Feb.	15 April	24 May	3 June	14 June	2 Dec.
2002	13 Feb.	31 March	9 May	19 May	30 May	1 Dec.
2003	5 March	20 April	29 May	8 June	19 June	30 Nov.
2004	25 Feb.	11 April	20 May	30 May	10 June	28 Nov.
2005	9 Feb.	27 March	5 May	15 May	26 May	27 Nov.
2006	1 March	16 April	25 May	4 June	15 June	3 Dec.
2007	21 Feb.	8 April	17 May	27 May	7 June	2 Dec.
2008	6 Feb.	23 March	1 May	11 May	22 May	30 Nov.
2009	25 Feb.	12 April	21 May	31 May	11 June	29 Nov.
2010	17 Feb.	4 April	13 May	23 May	3 June	28 Nov.
2011	9 March	24 April	2 June	12 June	23 June	27 Nov.
2012	22 Feb.	8 April	17 May	27 May	7 June	2 Dec.
2013	13 Feb.	31 March	9 May	19 May	30 May	1 Dec.
2014	5 March	20 April	29 May	8 June	19 June	30 Nov.
2015	18 Feb.	5 April	14 May	24 May	4 June	29 Nov.
2016	10 Feb.	27 March	5 May	15 May	26 May	27 Nov.
2017	1 March	16 April	25 May	4 June	15 June	3 Dec.
2018	14 Feb.	1 April	10 May	20 May	31 May	2 Dec.
2019	6 March	21 April	30 May	9 June	20 June	1 Dec.
2020	26 Feb.	12 April	21 May	31 May	11 June	29 Nov.
2021	17 Feb.	4 April	13 May	23 May	3 June	28 Nov.
2022	2 March	17 April	26 May	5 June	16 June	27 Nov.
2023	22 Feb.	9 April	18 May	28 May	8 June	3 Dec.
2024	14 Feb.	31 March	9 May	19 May	30 May	1 Dec.
2025	5 March	20 April	29 May	8 June	19 June	30 Nov.

TABLE EIGHT:
MOVABLE CHRISTIAN FESTIVALS (GREGORIAN CALENDAR)

	Ash Wednesday	Easter	Ascension	Pentecost	Corpus Christi	First Sunday in Advent
2026	18 Feb.	5 April	14 May	24 May	4 June	29 Nov.
2027	10 Feb.	28 March	6 May	16 May	27 May	28 Nov.
2028	2 March	16 April	25 May	4 June	15 June	3 Dec.
2029	14 Feb.	1 April	10 May	20 May	31 May	2 Dec.
2030	6 March	21 April	30 May	9 June	20 June	1 Dec.
2031	26 Feb.	13 April	22 May	1 June	12 June	30 Nov.
2032	11 Feb.	28 March	6 May	16 May	27 May	28 Nov.
2033	2 March	17 April	26 May	5 June	16 June	27 Nov.
2034	22 Feb.	9 April	18 May	28 May	8 June	3 Dec.
2035	7 Feb.	25 March	3 May	13 May	24 May	2 Dec.
2036	27 Feb.	13 April	22 May	1 June	12 June	30 Nov.
2037	18 Feb.	5 April	14 May	24 May	4 June	29 Nov.
2038	10 March	25 April	3 June	13 June	24 June	28 Nov.
2039	23 Feb.	10 April	19 May	29 May	9 June	27 Nov.
2040	15 Feb.	1 April	10 May	20 May	31 May	2 Dec.
2041	6 March	21 April	30 May	9 June	20 June	1 Dec.
2042	19 Feb.	6 April	15 May	25 May	5 June	30 Nov.
2043	11 Feb.	29 March	7 May	17 May	28 May	29 Nov.
2044	3 March	17 April	26 May	5 June	16 June	27 Nov.
2045	22 Feb.	9 April	18 May	28 May	8 June	3 Dec.
2046	7 Feb.	25 March	3 May	13 May	24 May	2 Dec.
2047	27 Feb.	14 April	23 May	2 June	13 June	1 Dec.
2048	19 Feb.	5 April	14 May	24 May	4 June	29 Nov.
2049	3 March	18 April	27 May	6 June	17 June	28 Nov.
2050	23 Feb.	10 April	19 May	29 May	9 June	27 Nov.
2051	15 Feb.	2 April	11 May	21 May	1 June	3 Dec.
2052	7 March	21 April	30 May	9 June	20 June	1 Dec.
2053	19 Feb.	6 April	15 May	25 May	5 June	30 Nov.
2054	11 Feb.	29 March	7 May	17 May	28 May	29 Nov.
2055	3 March	18 April	27 May	6 June	17 June	28 Nov.
2056	16 Feb.	2 April	11 May	21 May	1 June	3 Dec.

TABLE EIGHT:
MOVABLE CHRISTIAN FESTIVALS (GREGORIAN CALENDAR)

	Ash Wednesday	Easter	Ascension	Pentecost	Corpus Christi	First Sunday in Advent
2057	7 March	22 April	31 May	10 June	21 June	2 Dec.
2058	27 Feb.	14 April	23 May	2 June	13 June	1 Dec.
2059	12 Feb.	30 March	8 May	18 May	29 May	30 Nov.
2060	3 March	18 April	27 May	6 June	17 June	28 Nov.
2061	23 Feb.	10 April	19 May	29 May	9 June	27 Nov.
2062	8 Feb.	26 March	4 May	14 May	25 May	3 Dec.
2063	28 Feb.	15 April	24 May	3 June	14 June	2 Dec.
2064	20 Feb.	6 April	15 May	25 May	5 June	30 Nov.
2065	11 Feb.	29 March	7 May	17 May	28 May	29 Nov.
2066	24 Feb.	11 April	20 May	30 May	10 June	28 Nov.
2067	16 Feb.	3 April	12 May	22 May	2 June	27 Nov.
2068	7 March	22 April	31 May	10 June	21 June	2 Dec.
2069	27 Feb.	14 April	23 May	2 June	13 June	1 Dec.
2070	12 Feb.	30 March	8 May	18 May	29 May	30 Nov.
2071	4 March	19 April	28 May	7 June	18 June	29 Nov.
2072	24 Feb.	10 April	19 May	29 May	9 June	27 Nov.
2073	8 Feb.	26 March	4 May	14 May	25 May	3 Dec.
2074	28 Feb.	15 April	24 May	3 June	14 June	2 Dec.
2075	20 Feb.	7 April	16 May	26 May	6 June	1 Dec.
2076	4 March	19 April	28 May	7 June	18 June	29 Nov.
2077	24 Feb.	11 April	20 May	30 May	10 June	28 Nov.
2078	16 Feb.	3 April	12 May	22 May	2 June	27 Nov.
2079	8 March	23 April	1 June	11 June	22 June	3 Dec.
2080	21 Feb.	7 April	16 May	26 May	6 June	1 Dec.
2081	12 Feb.	30 March	8 May	18 May	29 May	30 Nov.
2082	4 March	19 April	28 May	7 June	18 June	29 Nov.
2083	17 Feb.	4 April	13 May	23 May	3 June	28 Nov.
2084	9 Feb.	26 March	4 May	14 May	25 May	3 Dec.
2085	28 Feb.	15 April	24 May	3 June	14 June	2 Dec.
2086	13 Feb.	31 March	9 May	19 May	30 May	1 Dec.
2087	5 March	20 April	29 May	8 June	19 June	30 Nov.

	Ash Wednesday	Easter	Ascension	Pentecost	Corpus Christi	First Sunday in Advent
2088	25 Feb.	11 April	20 May	30 May	10 June	28 Nov.
2089	16 Feb.	3 April	12 May	22 May	2 June	27 Nov.
2090	1 March	16 April	25 May	4 June	15 June	3 Dec.
2091	21 Feb.	8 April	17 May	27 May	7 June	2 Dec.
2092	13 Feb.	30 March	8 May	18 May	29 May	30 Nov.
2093	25 Feb.	12 April	21 May	31 May	11 June	29 Nov.
2094	17 Feb.	4 April	13 May	23 May	3 June	28 Nov.
2095	9 March	24 April	2 June	12 June	23 June	27 Nov.
2096	29 Feb.	15 April	24 May	3 June	14 June	2 Dec.
2097	13 Feb.	31 March	9 May	19 May	30 May	1 Dec.
2098	5 March	20 April	29 May	8 June	19 June	30 Nov.
2099	25 Feb.	12 April	21 May	31 May	11 June	29 Nov.
2100	11 Feb.	28 March	6 May	16 May	27 May	28 Nov.
2101	2 March	17 April	26 May	5 June	16 June	27 Nov.
2102	22 Feb.	9 April	18 May	28 May	8 June	3 Dec.
2103	7 Feb.	25 March	3 May	13 May	24 May	2 Dec.
2104	27 Feb.	13 April	22 May	1 June	12 June	30 Nov.
2105	18 Feb.	5 April	14 May	24 May	4 June	29 Nov.
2106	3 March	18 April	27 May	6 June	17 June	28 Nov.
2107	23 Feb.	10 April	19 May	29 May	9 June	27 Nov.
2108	15 Feb.	1 April	10 May	20 May	31 May	2 Dec.
2109	6 March	21 April	30 May	9 June	20 June	1 Dec.
2110	19 Feb.	6 April	15 May	25 May	5 June	30 Nov.
2111	11 Feb.	29 March	7 May	17 May	28 May	29 Nov.
2112	3 March	17 April	26 May	5 June	16 June	27 Nov.
2113	15 Feb.	2 April	11 May	21 May	1 June	3 Dec.
2114	7 March	22 April	31 May	10 June	21 June	2 Dec.
2115	27 Feb.	14 April	23 May	2 June	13 June	1 Dec.
2116	12 Feb.	29 March	7 May	17 May	28 May	29 Nov.
2117	3 March	18 April	27 May	6 June	17 June	28 Nov.
2118	23 Feb.	10 April	19 May	29 May	9 June	27 Nov.

Table Eight:
Movable Christian Festivals (Gregorian Calendar)

	Ash Wednesday	Easter	Ascension	Pentecost	Corpus Christi	First Sunday in Advent
2119	8 Feb.	26 March	4 May	14 May	25 May	3 Dec.
2120	28 Feb.	14 April	23 May	2 June	13 June	1 Dec.
2121	19 Feb.	6 April	15 May	25 May	5 June	30 Nov.
2122	11 Feb.	29 March	7 May	17 May	28 May	29 Nov.
2123	24 Feb.	11 April	20 May	30 May	10 June	28 Nov.
2124	16 Feb.	2 April	11 May	21 May	1 June	3 Dec..
2125	7 March	22 April	31 May	10 June	21 June	2 Dec.
2126	27 Feb.	14 April	23 May	2 June	13 June	1 Dec.
2127	12 Feb.	30 March	8 May	18 May	29 May	30 Nov.
2128	3 March	18 April	27 May	6 June	17 June	28 Nov.
2129	23 Feb.	10 April	19 May	29 May	9 June	27 Nov.
2130	8 Feb.	26 March	4 May	14 May	25 May	3 Dec.
2131	28 Feb.	15 April	24 May	3 June	14 June	2 Dec.
2132	20 Feb.	6 April	15 May	25 May	5 June	30 Nov.
2133	4 March	19 April	28 May	7 June	18 June	29 Nov.
2134	24 Feb.	11 April	20 May	30 May	10 June	28 Nov.
2135	16 Feb.	3 April	12 May	22 May	2 June	27 Nov.
2136	7 March	22 April	31 May	10 June	21 June	2 Dec.
2137	20 Feb.	7 April	16 May	26 May	6 June	1 Dec.
2138	12 Feb.	30 March	8 May	18 May	29 May	30 Nov.
2139	4 March	19 April	28 May	7 June	18 June	29 Nov.
2140	17 Feb.	3 April	12 May	22 May	2 June	27 Nov.
2141	8 Feb.	26 March	4 May	14 May	25 May	3 Dec.
2142	28 Feb.	15 April	24 May	3 June	14 June	2 Dec.
2143	13 Feb.	31 March	9 May	19 May	30 May	1 Dec.
2144	4 March	19 April	28 May	7 June	18 June	29 Nov.
2145	24 Feb.	11 April	20 May	30 May	10 June	28 Nov.
2146	16 Feb.	3 April	12 May	22 May	2 June	27 Nov.
2147	1 March	16 April	25 May	4 June	15 June	3 Dec.
2148	21 Feb.	7 April	16 May	26 May	6 June	1 Dec.
2149	12 Feb.	30 March	8 May	18 May	29 May	30 Nov.

	Ash Wednesday	Easter	Ascension	Pentecost	Corpus Christi	First Sunday in Advent
2150	25 Feb.	12 April	21 May	31 May	11 June	29 Nov.
2151	17 Feb.	4 April	13 May	23 May	3 June	28 Nov.
2152	8 March	23 April	1 June	11 June	22 June	3 Dec.
2153	28 Feb.	15 April	24 May	3 June	14 June	2 Dec.
2154	13 Feb.	31 March	9 May	19 May	30 May	1 Dec.
2155	5 March	20 April	29 May	8 June	19 June	30 Nov.
2156	25 Feb.	11 April	20 May	30 May	10 June	28 Nov.
2157	9 Feb.	27 March	5 May	15 May	26 May	27 Nov.
2158	1 March	16 April	25 May	4 June	15 June	3 Dec.
2159	21 Feb.	8 April	17 May	27 May	7 June	2 Dec.
2160	6 Feb.	23 March	1 May	11 May	22 May	30 Nov.
2161	25 Feb.	12 April	21 May	31 May	11 June	29 Nov.
2162	17 Feb.	4 April	13 May	23 May	3 June	28 Nov.
2163	9 March	24 April	2 June	12 June	23 June	27 Nov.
2164	22 Feb.	8 April	17 May	27 May	7 June	2 Dec.
2165	13 Feb.	31 March	9 May	19 May	30 May	1 Dec.
2166	5 March	20 April	29 May	8 June	19 June	30 Nov.
2167	18 Feb.	5 April	14 May	24 May	4 June	29 Nov.
2168	10 Feb.	27 March	5 May	15 May	26 May	27 Nov.
2169	1 March	16 April	25 May	4 June	15 June	3 Dec.
2170	14 Feb.	1 April	10 May	20 May	31 May	2 Dec.
2171	6 March	21 April	30 May	9 June	20 June	1 Dec.
2172	26 Feb.	12 April	21 May	31 May	11 June	29 Nov.
2173	17 Feb.	4 April	13 May	23 May	3 June	28 Nov.
2174	2 March	17 April	26 May	5 June	16 June	27 Nov.
2175	22 Feb.	9 April	18 May	28 May	8 June	3 Dec.
2176	14 Feb.	31 March	9 May	19 May	30 May	1 Dec.
2177	5 March	20 April	29 May	8 June	19 June	30 Nov.
2178	18 Feb.	5 April	14 May	24 May	4 June	29 Nov.
2179	10 Feb.	28 March	6 May	16 May	27 May	28 Nov.
2180	1 March	16 April	25 May	4 June	15 June	3 Dec.

MOVABLE CHRISTIAN FESTIVALS (GREGORIAN CALENDAR)

	Ash Wednesday	Easter	Ascension	Pentecost	Corpus Christi	First Sunday in Advent
2181	14 Feb.	1 April	10 May	20 May	31 May	2 Dec.
2182	6 March	21 April	30 May	9 June	20 June	1 Dec.
2183	26 Feb.	13 April	22 May	1 June	12 June	30 Nov.
2184	11 Feb.	28 March	6 May	16 May	27 May	28 Nov.
2185	2 March	17 April	26 May	5 June	16 June	27 Nov.
2186	22 Feb.	9 April	18 May	28 May	8 June	3 Dec.
2187	7 Feb.	25 March	3 May	13 May	24 May	2 Dec.
2188	27 Feb.	13 April	22 May	1 June	12 June	30 Nov.
2189	18 Feb.	5 April	14 May	24 May	4 June	29 Nov.
2190	10 May	25 April	3 June	13 June	24 June	28 Nov.
2191	23 Feb.	10 April	19 May	29 May	9 June	27 Nov.
2192	15 Feb.	1 April	10 May	20 May	31 May	2 Dec.
2193	6 March	21 April	30 May	9 June	20 June	1 Dec.
2194	19 Feb.	6 April	15 May	25 May	5 June	30 Nov.
2195	11 Feb.	29 March	7 May	17 May	28 May	29 Nov.
2196	2 March	17 April	26 May	5 June	16 June	27 Nov.
2197	22 Feb.	9 April	18 May	28 May	8 June	3 Dec.
2198	7 Feb.	25 March	3 May	13 May	24 May	2 Dec.
2199	27 Feb.	14 April	23 May	2 June	13 June	1 Dec.
2200	19 Feb.	6 April	15 May	25 May	5 June	30 Nov.
2201	4 March	19 April	28 May	7 June	18 June	29 Nov.
2202	24 Feb.	11 April	20 May	30 May	10 June	28 Nov.
2203	16 Feb.	3 April	12 May	22 May	2 June	27 Nov.
2204	29 Feb.	15 April	24 May	3 June	14 June	2 Dec.
2205	20 April	7 April	16 May	26 May	6 June	1 Dec.
2206	12 Feb.	30 March	8 May	18 May	29 May	30 Nov.
2207	25 Feb.	12 April	21 May	31 May	11 June	29 Nov.
2208	17 Feb.	3 April	12 May	22 May	2 June	27 Nov.
2209	8 March	23 April	1 June	11 June	21 June	3 Dec.
2210	3 March	18 April	27 May	6 June	17 June	28 Nov.
2211	13 Feb.	31 March	9 May	19 May	30 May	1 Dec.